ABOUT FACE

A·B·O·U·T
F·A·C·E

RACE IN POSTMODERN AMERICA

·

TIMOTHY MALIQALIM SIMONE

·

AUTONOMEDIA

AUTONOMEDIA
55 South 11th Street
POB 568
Brooklyn, NY
11211 USA

Printed in the United States of America.

Contents

ABOUT FACE

1

Race:
A Gnatty Persistence

❀ 1 ❀

EARLY IN THE FALL OF 1977, I SAT ON A ROAD TWO HOURS
northeast of Nouakchott, the capital of Mauritania in north-
west Africa, with Ali Malim, waiting for lorries scheduled
to bring relief food supplies. Ali Malim was a Hassani, a
former herder who—now in his 43rd year, with a family of
twelve—had no income, no camels. The drought that irrevocably leveled the graze-and-herd economy had done its
work. From all over the Shinqit, members of the Hassani,

the Peul, and some Tuareg were gravitating toward administrative centers to wait out their death. No anger, no mourning. Peoples that had made historical reputations out of their fierce cunning and adamant self-sufficiency were now indifferent to the absence of expectation and the inevitability of demise.

As Malim and I sat, saying little, a black man in European dress stepped from a car bearing an official insignia. Equipped with pen and clipboard, he was of probable Toucoleur origin. At the black man's arrival, Ali Malim, raised from his somnolence, became suddenly animated. "See this man," he pointed, "even when we will have nothing to eat, he will always have his blackness."

When I asked him what he meant, Ali Malim continued, "they know enough not to take all of this too seriously. They saw the trouble coming; they see everything, and, for this, they will be punished and punished more. It has always been impossible for us (the Hassani) to be like them, but it shouldn't stop us from trying."

The peculiar complexities of Mauritanian race relations aside, Ali Malim's remarks begin to navigate the overgrown and obdurate thickets of race with an understanding usually missing from the feigned assuredness of the academy. He acknowledges the inextricable interweaving of fear, resignation, admiration, carelessness and risk that has imbued the phenomena of race with a gnatty and troubling persistence. As a concept for thinking about and organizing the visible social world, the meaning of race has become increasingly clandestine, wrapping that which is visible in a network of epidermic invisibilities. Race has shifted from being the definitive categorizer—the means of separating the wheat from the chaff—to the necessary reminder that the real body, social and individual, is always elsewhere, just out of view. It is the instrument through which this body becomes perpetually unsettled, either too certain or uncertain as to how, exactly, it should take itself.

It is in race that the postmodern world today finds its most exemplary vanishing point. Race appears as if it is something fixed and permanent, immune to being altered by the ideas or expressions used to address or comprehend it. Yet, what does it really mean? To what extent does it have anything to say about specifiable differences between peoples, cultures and histories? The point here is that when we talk about race we are never sure what we are referring to: a dilemma which posits many contradictory futures and opportunities.

Throughout various historical periods, notions of race have demonstrated great versatility, operating as effectively in silence as in actual discourse. At times, race enables people to seem more different than they are; at other times, it makes people look more similar than is useful. It has been used to assure white people not to take blackness seriously, or to insist that they take blackness more seriously than it warrants. The logic of race both recklessly includes and excludes, overvalues and undervalues, affirms and denies. This recklessness is a fundamental aspect of its appeal and of the passions it generates—the quick, careless certainty it provides to a swirling, ambiguous social field.

Even though race is probably best apprehended and understood in specific instances, my effort here is less on trying to understand the meaning and use of race per se as it is to review and conceive of ways to talk about it, talk through it. I focus on how to feel it, attend to and ignore it, how to affiliate and engage with it without necessarily having to understand it. I am particularly interested in how race applies to the future of white and black relations in the United States.

In making race sensible, there is an implicit danger in attempting to overcome its mystery by reducing it to rational constructs. The incessant obsession to rationalize may be a symptom of a faltering social imagination, an imagination necessary for conceiving of new ways for whites and blacks to be together. Race may constitute the last outpost of such rational comprehension itself, and may be rejuvenated by each new, fledgling attempt to speak its truth as the prerequisite for killing it off. Frustrated, we then ineluctably attempt to stop speaking about it—a move which also prolongs its vitality. It is precisely the need to comprehend the dynamics of race fully that generates much of the contemporary behavior that can be appropriately construed as racist, because such a need often curtails the willingness of whites to engage with blacks. Even the slipperiness of the definition and use of the term "racist" promises to confound whatever conceptual conviction is achieved.

The message in Ali Malim's words is that the impossibility of comprehending race should not deter whites from being moved and influenced by blacks. In the long run it is in this—a refusal or inability to be moved—that race exerts its most forceful effects. This refusal generates a practice of racialism, where race is used as an instrument to constitute social bodies as fixed to specific sites, patterns of mobility, and experiences of social exchange. Albeit dangerous and fraught with the renewal of overt racial discord, only when white people can become indifferent to the risks of their full (and, perhaps, possible) immersion in a broad range of meanings produced by race, will there be a transformation in white/black interactions. Fears and attractions, the lofty and the petty, the rational and the insane, must all be articulated at once.

Their struggles have secured for African Americans legal, if not actual, access to the full breadth of American socioeconomic and cultural life. But the empowerment of black aspirations and the uncurtailed development of black life increasingly entails the willingness and ability of whites to consider African Americans as having something significant to offer their own lives. Will the experiences, histories, and cultural productions of African Americans be deemed essential references for the educational and psychological development of all Americans? This essay considers what whites will have to know, both about themselves and about African Americans, if this learning is to have a chance.

❧ 2 ❧

I HAVE SEVERAL MOTIVES FOR INITIATING THIS DISCUSSION. I have been engaged in a wide range of affiliations with black people all my life. In these affiliations, nothing has ever been clear. The closer the proximity, the more intensified both their loving and their despising have become. Although

I have been included within the interior of black life more than most white people, the inclusion results, at times, in a kind of exclusion inaccessible to almost all other whites. The more I attempt to go back and forth between white and black worlds, the more precarious I feel; both the danger and safety are maximized. Repeatedly I have heard, "what the fuck is a white man doing over here?" It is a statement directed to me, but formed linguistically for an imaginary third party—a means of circumventing a direct confrontation. Seldom is my presence pursued, nor am I attacked or ignored. Rather, I am let go by their own bewilderment. There are no unequivocable emotions; what you end up being accepted or despised for becomes just as unclear for blacks as it is for you, the white.

Walking recently, with a thoroughly chadorred black woman friend, to a coffee shop on busy Utica Avenue on a torrid summer day in Brooklyn, I anticipated the expression of strong emotions. But I had not anticipated the intense and simultaneous resiliency and obduracy of the confusion generated by me—a white muslim—accompanying a black muslim woman. A religion which, in America, has provided a basis for the exclusion of white by black, became, in this instance, the only available means to justify our presence together.

In the coffee shop, this alliance became the subject of great debate. Threats were made, but quickly and just as vigorously withdrawn. One man insisted, "You must marry her now, quickly." Something which at one time I had very much wanted to do, but dismissed out of fear, was now being proposed as a punishment for our indiscretion. A small crowd had gathered outside—something was being proven, demonstrated, but no one knew what or why.

Other incidents, involving non-Islamic black women, had been much more clear-cut; the woman is chastised, mocked, or—more recently—understood in her pragmatism, "it's like that these days isn't it sis, isn't it." Increasingly, there is a greater uncertainty over what to make of interracial encounters and affiliations.

On holidays I sit with my relatives, my black wife present, and listen to them still talk about "the welfare cases, the people who screw, have babies, and don't do any work." We then go to her relatives, where the talk is about "the white man who talks nothing but shit." In both situations the food and warmth are plentiful. Yet, there are no overt comments, no efforts made to acknowledge that either a white man or a black woman is now part of the family. In other situations of this type there are usually apologies or remedial qualification ("I hope you don't take this personally"; "I'm only talking in general"; "All of them but you"; "You know we like you, but..."). It is not that either my wife or I demand that such a statistically improbable event as our relationship deserves any extraordinary comment. Too often the focus on such events detracts attention from the continuous and systematic repression of such relationships and merely feeds the fascination for the discursive: something to talk about without having to deal with the impact of the thing spoken. Such discussions tend to disproportionately highlight the ameliorative trends or capacities of the larger society, make it seem like "there is no problem," or that "things are getting better." Rather, what is disturbing in the absence of acknowledgement is that our togetherness is viewed as having no distinguishing force, no impact except to trigger a marginalization from kin which must, in turn, be necessarily accommodated.

Once, while making a visit to some intimate white friends who had gathered for a dinner party, I stepped out to run a quick errand only to discover, after less than a minute, that my money was in an overcoat I had left inside the apartment. Just upon entering the door, I heard one of my friends say to the others, "You know, I just hope he cools out with all that black shit, I'm tired of hearing it. What does he expect me to do, give up my life for them?" Although I had shared a long and troubled political history with all the people inside, I did not or had not advocated that any of them do anything in this regard.

What is apparent to me is that race increasingly involves the question of what can be legitimately talked about, and how. It entails a discursive politics concerning what can be said and done about human differences. Much of America's explicit racial vocabulary has been retired; many of the same points are being made, but in a different language, under a different guise. Neither whites nor blacks want to hear about whiteness and blackness, not because racial differences signify any less, or that race has declined in importance, but because people just don't want to deal with it. Part of this reluctance stems from an attitude—as expressed recently by one of my cousins—that "all the talk about it doesn't change anything, so maybe it's best to just leave it alone."

In the aftermath of the civil rights movement of the

sixties and seventies, American culture has discovered that racial effects are more efficiently achieved in a language cleansed of overt racial reference. Although conceptual precision in discussions about American social life demands that racial discourse employ racial categories, such categories may or may not make explicit reference to perceivable and acknowledgeable racial characteristics such as skin color. Instead, they employ more subtle signifiers: "street youths," "welfare mothers," "inner-city residents." With the broad recognition that racial discourse may not necessarily produce racist effects—or may not produce them with anything like the proficiency of seemingly non-racial discourse—the terrain is established for the pervasive avoidance of any explicit reference to sociocultural differences historically related to race. Ushered into the eighties is a generalized reluctance to speak in black and white. As I will discuss later, such a temerity may rehabilitate and reinvigorate racist operations.

HERE IS AN ADDITIONAL MOTIVATION FOR THIS DISCUSSION OF race. I believe there are concepts and strategies located in black practices of signification that forcefully address and pose suggestions for living through the redefinitions of self, intelligence, and freedom currently taking place within "postmodern" Western culture. Here, "practices of signification" refers to the extralinguistic processes whereby selves and peoples, peculiarly inscribed within a series of overlapping intrapersonal, political, and cultural contexts, attempt to understand their relationships with various others and with themselves (Geertz 1973, 1983; Kristeva 1975, 1980). In other words, there is something about how meaning is produced and used in various parts of the Black World that is eminently important for white lives today. In the past, Negri (1980) has forcefully examined the means through which people of color have been the subject of history, have shaped the cultural parameters of the Western world through their struggles to mediate the forms of oppression used against them. Now, in an era of world telecommunications, Western precepts and cognitive orientations themselves dictate the applicability of black worldviews.

I do not wish to discuss the specific ways such an intersection of cultural forms and worldviews would produce a re-rendering of Western orientations. My interest is to discuss the factors which operate to prevent this interpenetration and dialogue from taking place. Although the specifics of such applications do exist, the idea of the interchange itself must be considered significant outside the particulars of the evidence. An openness to supplementing the conventional means for achieving understanding, an openness for elaborating what is considered feasible behavior, and an openness for empowering African American world views, are necessary prerequisites to this critical scrutiny of the Black World.

Teaching at a black college for the past seven years, I have found that my willingness as a white man to be moved, swayed, and influenced by my students' consciously invoked blackness has been the key element in enabling some unanticipated form of sociality and dialogue to emerge. That such influence occurs remains crucial, but it is secondary to this willingness.

AN INTRINSIC ASPECT OF THIS WILLINGNESS TO BE MOVED IS A willingness to acknowledge the existence of a Black World constituted by Africa and blacks in the diaspora. Such acknowledgement for white Americans involves their willingness to accord validity and importance to ideas and expressive forms outside the purview of white interpretive frameworks—a willingness to see meaning where before the only meaning obtainable was a deficient version of white processes. More importantly, it entails an acceptance of forms of cultural input, value, and solidarity that exceed the white American experience and, for the most part, is currently unavailable to it. Equally important is the implicit admission by whites that there might be something happening in their midst that is simply not theirs to know yet.

The use of the designation "Black World" is not meant to imply the existence of a coherent cultural view, an assemblage of political interests, a distinct psychology, or a mode of polity based on race. It is used here to make broad reference to the interlinkages of the political fates of black people, an acknowledgement of worldwide racism. The designation also reflects an increasing emphasis by black scholars for constituting new fields of interpretation and for forging areas of common political interest, particularly in light of attenuations in the physical and cultural distances that have in the past rendered historical aspirations for such linkages problematic.

Stack (1981) sees viability and saliency in the designation "Black World" as a means of denoting a transnational ethnic and a cultural domain that play an intermediate role in the time period between the demise of the state system and the institution of a homogeneous global political culture. Rosenau (1981) warns of an accelerating disaggregation of traditional collectivities accompanying the cascading interdependence of basic political and economic functions. Individuals, he says—regardless of national, cultural, or class background—increasingly define themselves as global actors. They explain the events of their lives through more elaborate, transterritorial causal chains. Subsequently, they identify with collective forms that most clearly define their needs and aspirations and compensate for their perceived loss of control over the course of individual and social events. Collective aggregates based on a common blackness may attain great importance, especially now that Black America sees itself under renewed attack, and as contacts with African and Caribbean peoples become more widespread.

Being the object of attack, however, has historically been the very thing which has cohered a Black World once it "exceeded" its African borders. Uya (1982) argues that from the 15th century, the entirety of the Black World has been the target and object of transformation by the Western world. Slavery, colonialism, segregation, and postcolonial underdevelopment and selfdenial are to be viewed as aspects of an overarching logic of uneven development under global capitalism—a logic for undermining the Black World. This logic has uprooted and dispersed blacks and has elicited a wide range of strategies, adjustments, resistances, and complicities that are rendered sensible and connectable only by viewing attacks against blacks in this larger, global framework.

Even though the Beni, Djuka, and Saramanka of the Guyanas, the apalençados and acquilombolas of Brazil, the Haitian guerrilleros and Jamaican maroons all produced different cultural responses to their liberation from direct white rule during the 17th to 19th centuries, this heterogeneity—far from detracting from a sense of commonality and connectedness—elaborated the generative and creative capacities of African peoples to develop under a wide variety of conditions. Additionally, as Skinner (1982) points out, the history of Black America is a history of compatibility between aspirations for and actualization of American citizenship and African identification. Although denials of commonality and intercultural tensions do exist (for example, between West Indians and Black Americans), such tensions seem to occur when an American identification is prioritized over blackness; when immigrant groups, anxious to shake their third world status, fail to see how their own economic behavior and aspirations implicitly contribute to a third world status for Black Americans. What starts out as a difference in relative wage and currency value—i.e., poor wages in the U.S. are relatively high wages when converted into Caribbean currencies—gets transformed into a range of sociocultural conflicts because these wages are unacceptable to Black Americans.

❁ 5 ❁

IS THERE A ROLE FOR A DYNAMIC AFRICANITY? IN THIS ERA, according to Noack (1983), even such a question may serve to undermine a place for such a notion. The discrepancy between that which is and that which is necessary becomes increasingly wide. The postmodern need for incessant innovation requires that such innovation be planned long in advance of its appearance. The quality of that planning, then, becomes suspect and irreversible, ill-equipped to address unanticipated trends and contingencies. The resultant crises are deferred to other situations, making it difficult for anyone to understand what is occurring. With the incessant production of new evidence, new images, new references, and new factors—all announcing themselves as significant, all demanding attention—individuals and societies find it almost impossible to make important decisions.

If Western culture is to continue, says Noack, there will be a need for new forms of coherency, however provisional they may be. Gone are the days of stable superegos that permit refined and leisurely judgements. Gone are the longitudinal research protocols that determine and achieve maximum levels of consonance between the preferred strategies and our cherished values. The erosion of fundamental boundaries (child/adult, private/public, high culture/low culture) and the often apparent seamlessness of Western social stratification make it difficult for individuals to know precisely where they stand and, therefore, what the anticipated outcomes and ramifications of any decision might be.

Adaptation now means adeptness in quickly revising identities and trading in whatever one can get one's hands on. Calinescu (1982) chimes in: "even the most incompatible ideas or theories are dialogically compatible by virtue of simply being presented as alternative solutions to similar, although never quite identical problems." (274)

The African experience, despite the cautionary warnings of Noack, might provide some ideas on how to address these postmodern anxieties. For example, consider the use of rhetorical edification during the postcolonial period. This consisted of ways of talking about possible futures full of quickly drawn images, citations, and identities in invocational, sermon-like formats which were intended to suggest grounds or paradigms for the gradual recuperation of a sense of collective belonging that had been vitiated under colonial rule (Fernandez 1978, 1980). Fragments of cultural memory, idiomatic sayings, and pieces of verse—all decontextualized from their original functions—are offered up again in anticipation that the collective can weave together an operational coherency. This re-emphasis on proverbial idioms was viewed as a means of healing and of reconciling the fragmented and uprooted individual with a larger sense of communal identity. Unlike the spirit entailed in these African edification rituals, the postmodern sentiment is: when you make yourself, you have to stop at nothing less than making the whole world, so when you belong to the world, you merely belong to yourself. Without a "real" world, the self consumes itself in a circuit of fascination and disgust.

The North's force-feeding of the South with its cultural and media products can be viewed as a desperate attempt by the North to avoid any assessment anywhere of the value, use, and meaning of the information produced and transferred (Mattelart et al. 1984). It is an attempt to drown out all other voices, so that the heritage of Western culture may be retained by default. So even though the Western individual recognizes the need to turn elsewhere for sources of fresh input, s/he still needs to do all the talking.

IN CONSIDERING THE WHITE USE OF BLACK WORLDVIEWS, THE issue of race reasserts itself in both old and new ways. In order to learn from blackness, race must inevitably be considered by whites. Even if it is put aside as an impediment to the absorption and assimilation of black ideas, values, and sensibilities, the issue of race returns to challenge the nature of the learning. It challenges by posing a series of difficult questions: Is a new form of parasitism taking place? Is the assumption of black ideas and worldviews simply a virulent means of recuperating white identity, so that it may resuscitate a waning confidence in its legitimacy to dominate others? Are ideas, sensibilities, and worldviews—when disembodied from the cultural, political, and historical situations which generated them—applicable to those outside the specificity of these cultural situations, to those who have had no prior experience with them? How are whites going to acquire this experience? If an apparatus of racial domination continues to exist, the learning borders on becoming a forced extraction. Is what is shown by blacks what is really believed in? This latter question stems from Césaire's (1983) point that if a person or culture perceives that they exist under oppression, they view whatever knowledge is gained about them as a means of incorporating them into the mainstream. Thus, they are compelled to embody that which is significant to them in what, to others, would be despised or construed as pathological. If this is the case, then do white Americans commence a general hunt for the "bad nigger" thinking that such a character is merely a disguise for ultimate wisdom?

These are tricky questions, difficult if not impossible to answer. There are many precedents and grounds for the concerns delineated by them. As Fanon pointed out nearly thirty years ago, the acknowledged contributions of blacks almost necessitate the overlay of racism in order to provide them their significance. Although the suffering and struggles of black people in slavery and emancipation are a vital part of the formation of Black culture and psyche, it seems, at times, that blacks are valued only for this suffering. If there had not been slavery, oppression, and struggle, there would not seem to be very much of value in the black experience. Whites in the United States have little appreciation for the heterogeneity and breadth of the black experience. When sympathetic or attentive, the focus of white interest tends to be on the depth of black victimage and suffering, the identification of exceptions to stereotypes, or the need to find and insist upon areas of commonality rather than in viewing that experience as having something of value to offer their own lives.

Until recently, a struggle-and-siege emphasis dominated most literature on black psychology. Most depictions of black psyche concentrated on one or more of the following characterizations:

¶ as the internalization of overt and institutional violence directed against it (Greer and Cobbs, 1969; Thomas and Sillen, 1972);

¶ as the incorporation and subsequent exaggeration of white mores and social attitudes (Fredricksen, 1972; McCulloch, 1983);

¶ as individual guilt in the face of relative social impotence in undoing the parameters of racial oppression, resulting in attacks upon the self and, thus, upon the constraints which deter violence being directed toward others (Greer and Cobbs, 1969; Wyne *et al.*, 1974);

¶ as organizational cohesion in the domestic unit, achieved through a necessity induced by constant crisis, where the household huddles together in a collective defense against 1) a successive chain of disruptive events, and 2) the prospects that any individual household member might exceed the status of any other member in terms of either economic or educational achievement (Christmas, 1973; Jenkins, 1982);

¶ as the ability to absorb suffering (Christmas, 1973; Hendin, 1969);

¶ as the difficulty in perceiving oneself as good and loving (Baughman, 1971; Hauser, 1971);

¶ as the rejection of Africanity in the imagination

(Gordon, 1977; Gladwin and Saiden, 1980); and as

¶ the assumption of deviance as adaptive behavior (Jenkins, 1982; Thomas and Sillen, 1972).

Although each of these characterizations has been an accurate description of many black persons in this country, such concepts tend to massify the black experience, to suggest that racism in this country has been so pernicious as to make it unlikely for blacks to obtain the level of psychological functioning adequate to their aspirations.

That there has been exploitation, and that this exploitation has had a profound effect on blacks, should not be played down or ignored. Neither should it, however, be allowed to totally dominate the consideration of the black experience. There has been and will be something else that will exceed this reality. The emphasis on exploitation leads too easily to the attitude, "well, since you people have proven you can take it, make a life out of it, why shouldn't you be the ones to assume the burden (whatever it is) now."

If whites eventually come to place greater value on black thoughts and experiences, a sense of universalism must be evoked, one that "resides in the decision to recognize and accept the reciprocal relativism of different cultures, once the colonial status is irreversibly excluded." (Fanon 1967, 447). Contemporary administrative and corporate forms seek to bury difference. They are ready to proclaim that only exemplary and optimum performance or competence now matters, regardless of sex or ethnicity, deftly ignoring that such competence must be nurtured. In this omission, we return to a state where competence is a matter of biological endowment even though we're supposedly not talking this language any more. All of a sudden, American society has discovered the virtues of equality. Everyone must be treated equally even though the ramifications of a legacy of inequality have produced a situation where long-term remedial efforts are necessary to make this nascent equality accessible to everyone. After centuries of denying any basic similarity between us and the "them" of the Third World, the new corporate logic emphasizes that various cultures are basically the same. The differences, if significant, are attributed to developmental lags, i.e., the formerly "backward" are in the process of almost catching up any minute now, so it's best to leave well enough alone.

One finds in the social sciences a renewal of an antirelativist position where Western man, unable to deal with the implications of a decentered identity, attempts to restore his predominance through discourses that tie together all cultural differences as simply variations of fundamental truths and moralities fronted as universal but thoroughly identified with the West. Wary of the implicit challenges offered by the Third World to Western cultural and technological achievements, America wants to feel at home everywhere, wants everywhere to be its home.

Implicit in the structural obsession with playing equality by the book (e.g., the attenuation of affirmative action programs; the lessons of fiscal responsibility schoolmarmed by the IMF) is the threat of expendability: "If you don't play it our way then who cares?". Decreasingly the feared, the despised, or the envied other, the useful slave or the source of cheap labor, what do blacks now become?

Specifically, the question is one of how blackness is

to be related to the apprehension of specific black persons, their characters, behaviors, and thoughts. One must be careful neither to lavish unwarranted praise or scorn. Blacks are perfectly capable of being arrogant parodies of inflated grandiosity or shaded apparitions of colonial nightmares. When whites can identify the same flaws in black personality that they find in themselves, does this mean that racial distinctions have become superfluous? A common theme these days is that "everyone is fucked up," everyone faces an everyday life filled with endless anxiety and uncertainty. No one can be excused. The message is: pervasive despair renders the old distinctions and antagonisms anachronistic.

In a culture where everyone, as Baudrillard (1982) points out, is minoritized (turned into a minority of one), there is no special status available: either everyone or no one is oppressed. As guilt is increasingly incorporated as a major facet of white identity, there is no reason to get rid of that guilt, no reason to feel guilty about the situation of others when basically all situations are the same. Within this framework, equality tends to connote expendability. If the differences between white and black are minimal or basically non-existent, why should whites be bothered with blacks? I believe that such attitudes are clearly dangerous, for they tend to promote psychological delinkages among people, and the suspicion that other people are potentially vulturous competitors or parasites interested only in using or being used. Equipped with this attitude about others, the individual finds it easy to justify his indifference.

❊ 7 ❊

WHAT IS URGENTLY NEEDED IS A RENEWED ETHNOGRAPHY OF racial and cultural difference. The feigned stance of universalism and the simulations of equality coincide with and contribute to an increasing separation of white and black worlds. Despite the increase in white–black contacts and the substantiation of a black middle class, the differences between white and black speech, economic position, and residential location have increased rather than diminished. Accompanying this separation is a greater indifference expressed by both worlds to the other, an indifference by both whites and blacks to engage with each other. The city becomes more of a closed system: entire sections and neighborhoods become virtually inaccessible to whites and their policing agents. Whites take their domiciles to the upper stories or into rural areas off the street, protected by sheer distance or expensive security systems. All of this occurs at the same moment in which the world becomes more like a large city, transversable in a matter of hours, connectable in a matter of seconds. Yet, for the most part, the Upper East Side and Brownsville in New York City seem light years apart, even though when I am compelled to enumerate and elaborate the differences, I often don't know what to say or where to begin. One neighborhood is primarily white, the other black; one rich and one poor. Although such distinctions explain much in terms of popular imagery or common sense, I am not sure in the long run what they really explain or account for.

The issues entailed by race require new forms of inquiry. Questions must be posed from a new position, one allowing that which is looked at to have a bearing on the questioner, to affect his/her life. An implication of Jules Rosette's (1978) research on Zairean religious movements is that the researcher's own presence in the Black World must become an object of inquiry.

Not many whites really know black life well enough to draw any conclusions about it. The reluctance of modern academics to engage with it is not too dissimilar from the reluctance of early "venture capitalists" in Africa who initially were afraid to travel inland from the Guinea coast. Today, whites are engaged with black sectors mainly to police, train, cure, or maintain them. The researcher must stop being purely a researcher if she is going to learn anything. In my time I have been teacher, confidant, criminal, drug abuser, muslim, religious novitiate, lover, "uncle," and comrade at funerals, weddings, birthdays, and sweet sixteen parties. Contrary to the common assumption, there are both public and private forums, arenas, and spaces accessible for these intersections. You won't always be liked, and you'll often feel uncomfortable. But, hell, where doesn't a person feel these things today.

The point is not to arrive at a new totality or synthesis; not to merge white and black into some new cosmic race along the lines of Vasconcellos, the early Hispanic scholar, or, more recently, Hoetink (1979). As whites change, blacks will change. It will be important that each not consider this reciprocity as a vehicle to greater autonomy or salvation, but rather an influence like any other. In each, the other will find stories, modes of action, styles of thought, ways of being, emotions, gaps, and silences to be used or not used—input to evaluate other input, itself evaluated, revised, and at one time accepted, at another, perhaps not. The task of ethnography is to prepare people for the suspension of their own common sense; it must convey meanings to whites that whites are convinced would make sense to blacks, and vice-versa (Marcus and Cushman 1982). Differences must be acknowledged, but the differences must not be articulated as emanating from a great and inherent separation between white and black worlds. Rather, the differences must be posited as provisionally occupiable and assumable by either side.

The Black World is many things. It has undergone multiple historical transformations, in which it has been fragmented and unified: unified indirectly through the common experience of fragmentation; fragmented in its inability to exert influence in the world capitalist system, as well as by the tendencies of others and itself to see it as one thing. Even Africans themselves possess a certain blindness in their inability to acknowledge the pervasive presence of Blacks in the Americas. When confronted with African Americans in their home territories, an almost pathological refusal to acknowledge the American ancestry of the African American frequently occurs.

Although it is equipped with a rich and substantial cultural legacy, the Black World takes its own vitality not from its "exoticism" but rather from its ability to extend and transform itself in multiple ways (as evidenced most elegantly by maroon cultures in the Americas, Price 1978;

the Kongo religious movements, Jules-Rosette 1978, 1979, 1980 and Fabian 1971; and slave-quarters culture, Webber 1978 and Genovese 1972). The Basic spirits may be shared among the various regions, nations, and ethnicities, but there is great diversity and range of cultural imagination, even though, as Drake (1982) indicates, the Black World has come increasingly to share its primary collective symbols. This heterogeneity has simultaneously been the Black World's strength and weakness, for it created the fluxus for both a successful introjection of colonial impositions and the grounds for continuous resistance against them. Subsequently, a fundamental aspect of both the social and personal was perceived to remain and develop outside the external system of Western control (Apostel 1981). The West consolidated its own cultural plurality but, then, refused to let go, refused to pluralize itself further. In Europe and North America, the defense of Western values is still important, even though few observers are able to say precisely what these values are and where they can be found.

The point of sameness and difference between white and black worlds is finally a political one. "Evidence" exists to make determinations of either essential sameness or difference sensible and valid; it is a matter of which is chosen and for what purposes. Either choice has many implications.

RACE HOVERS OVER AND IMPREGNATES EVERY ASPECT OF THIS choosing. Racial ideas, feelings, and discourses may exist solely to be applied in, through, and against the moment in which we choose what to pay attention to as sources of information and nurturance. It operates against our sense that we even have the ability to choose what our lives will look like. Instead, the outcome is seen as the evolution of some natural or overarching historical force over which we have little control. Additionally, a racial apparatus may re-inforce in us the sense that the act of choosing is insignifi-cant. No matter whether we choose to value individuals of other cultures or not, see approachable intersections or in-defatigable separation, we often resign ourselves to con-cluding that we are the products of our families and social upbringing. Too often the message of families, schools, media is: there is nothing in the Black World of any cul-tural or psychological value for the cultivation of white minds. White minds have no choice in this matter if they are to be functional, intelligent, and healthy.

A people which perceives that it has no choice about who and what will shape the fundamental contours of its existence, its ideas and feelings (even though in every re-spect peoples and cultures may move and shape it just as much through denial as through acceptance) will look upon itself as having to be what it presently is. Some people then hunger for change, obsessively pointing out the need for revision. Yet there is to be no change in this life, even though something beyond what is currently experienced is imagined and lived for. There are "beyonds" all over the place, but effort is still expended to stay in place. Deprived of the input of others, the people without choice fix them-selves to their present way of life and feel constantly inadequate. As inadequate, they feel threatened by the appearance of different peoples and alternative ways of living. These differences are alternately over-valued and devalued— anything to prevent taking them for what they are. The power to define oneself plus all others becomes a matter of self-preservation for a people who can find and place themselves only through these definitions. The notion of self becomes equated with self-defense—a defense of personal space, the space of an inviolable selfhood that, perhaps, no longer exists. Subsequently, when others speak, their speech can only be construed as an attempt to replace, compete, or deceive. The Other's voice must be silenced. The temptation to allow themselves to be swallowed up, in this other existence they desperately want to make their own, must be resisted. As a result, those Others are seen as hating them, resenting them, jealous of them. Accordingly, people without choice feel they have made the right choice after all.

HISTORICALLY, THIS BELIEF IN THE ABSENCE OF CHOICE HAS played a significant part in the creation of a racial apparatus. It is especially important with the advent of a postmodern administrative self—a form of personal identity where conventionality is submerged in favor of the presentation of fashionable subjectivities which display conventional connotations. The postmodern self feels she has endless choices available to her. Such endless choosing produces interminable cognitive dissonance which is resolved only by the individual doing her best to act like everyone else, i.e., be as similarly different as possible. The message is: you'll fit in as long as you're trying your best not to.

This process coincides with what Reeves (1983) calls ideological de-racialisation. De-racialisation is a process where racialist effects are exerted and racialist policies justified through a suspension of racial mention and an ambiguation of racist intention and prescription. What is produced is a racial discourse that obscures recognition of and attention to the full range of racial exploitations: moral blame is transferred from the perpetrators of acts and policies to the victims, who are re-labeled to mask the real level through which differences are organized. Immigrants, but not blacks, become the target, even though in the British context from which Reeves writes most immigrants are black. Where racialist discourse is not the sole producer of racialist effects, it becomes exceedingly difficult to assign moral judgement and determine whether construable racialist actions were obtained from clearly evident racial sentiments or intentions.

Since imputations of racism are highly charged discursive events that disrupt current emphases on acceptable public presentation and the deflection of anger and criticism, there is a general reluctance to see and ascribe racism. Such ascription becomes more difficult when it is less clear what is racist and what is not. The end result is an "improvement" in racialist effects. The discursive vehicles through which such effects could be identified and resisted are undermined. In a matter of years, Western culture has come a long way from propagating racism as "a doctrine

that a man's behavior is determined by stable inherited characteristics deriving from separate racial stocks having distinct attributes and usually considered to stand to one another in relations of superiority and inferiority" (Banton
1977). White Americans have moved from a position of felt
superiority to blacks to a position of surfeity.

They claim that they have attempted to connect and
integrate, and yet find meaningful contact and affiliations
impossible or too difficult, because American life just doesn't
nurture interracial contact. Additionally, racism increasingly
operates through practices where a category or group of
people can be abjected or ignored by referring to their individual personalities: e.g., "I'm this type of person and she's
that type." At the same time, such personal qualities can be
negated because the other person is a member of a general
category of types which tend to exclude a given individual
of a certain ethnic background—regardless of personality—
from substantive interaction with that group of people: i.e.,
"It's not that I refuse to deal with her, it's just that, being
who she is, she will not want to deal with me; I've got
nothing against her, it's just that a relationship is impossible given the circumstances." Here, racism operates through
a claim of impossibility in an American context which,
otherwise, sees everything as possible.

As people perceive that they have an extensive range
of personal and cultural choices available to them, the operation of a racial apparatus becomes more clandestine and
pervasive. People seize this supposed freedom as an opportunity to not have to deal with troubling issues. Thus, there
is a diminution of social obligation and sociality in general.

Sectors of individual and social life heretofore thought to be outside the scope of racialist operations are affected. We must keep in mind that there has not been a substantial increase in the amount or kinds of transformative choices available. Our "150-channel lives" not withstanding, there are few indications that people generally feel they can do many different things with their lives. The prohibitions and refusals have become more intricate, silent, and internalized. Yet, it is in this issue of choosing that a legacy of racism continues to be identified; it is the vehicle through which the initial and early contact with the Black World and our present postmodern culture can be connected. One need only ask the question, "can a white person choose to be black," in order to realize the saliency of this issue of choosing.

2

Fearing the Imagination

❖ 10 ❖

TWELFTH-CENTURY EUROPE WAS CAPTIVATED BY THE CORRE-
spondence of a mythological Ethiopian king named Prester
John, a person with whom many were already familiar from
the ethnographies of John Mandeville, who originally had
placed his kingdom in the Asian axis. In a continuation of
ancient myth, Prester John's desert kingdom was a virtual
paradise; poverty, thievery, adultery, and avarice were totally absent. The Ethiopians (a designation deriving from

the Greek *aithiops,* meaning "burnt face") were considered a people of priestly stature. Indeed, in the writing of the time the virtues of the Ethiopians were widely celebrated—excepting, of course, their color (Saunders 1978). The denial of color can be initially attributed to the fact that, from the late Roman empire on, the predominant image of blacks had changed from warrior to slave, although, according to Saunders, a positive image of blackness existed among the ancients even during the progressive enslavement of Africans.

Most Arab traders and adventurers assumed a much more negative view of blackness at the time, but it is doubtful that they even had their eyes open and, thus, produced an equally mythological—albeit inverted—form of that which dominated the European imagination. Ibn Haukal, from Baghdad, for example, traveled to Ghana in the twelfth century, and wrote, "I have not described the country of the African blacks and other peoples of the torrid zone because naturally loving wisdom, ingenuity, religion, justice, how could I notice such people as these, or magnify them by inserting an account of their country" (quoted in Saunders 1978). Those that kept their eyes open, such as Ibn Battuta in the Mali Kingdom, described the Africans as exceedingly just and fair.

When Europe's "great beyond" was finally "apprehended" in the sixteenth century, the kingdom of Prester John, Ethiopia, was found to be nothing like Europe had imagined it. Confronted was a barren land inhospitable to Western ways and values, and more significantly, dreams. Despite the demystification of this heaven on earth, part of the urgency to convert Africans into commodities (besides using slaves as a ruse to cover up the gold trade in Guinea) was the need to vitiate a power and knowledge that both terrified and impressed the early Western emissaries. There are many tales of the initial European inability to confront Africans head-on, face-to-face, in war and trading situations. Common are the confessions of deviousness, of deceit, of killing Africans when their backs were turned. For even though European visions of mortal salvation could not be actualized in Africa—and perhaps constituted a motivation for revenge, as manifested through the subsequent enslavement and colonization of African peoples—an ethos and cosmological age was discovered in Africa that profoundly disturbed Western minds.

Elias (1978) and Cohen (1980) remind us that Western society's expansionist tendencies between 1530–1720 were, themselves, compensations for Europe's own fundmental anxieties, hardships, and doubts. Europe had not fully or successfully repressed the behavioral displays it supposedly found rampant and so disturbing in Africa, i.e., public sex, public excretion, the absence of bodily inhibitions. Personhood and redemption were aspects of self-conception still nascent to European cognition. Religious grounds had to be solidified in order to enforce the system of penances, obligations, self-denials, and sacrifices that would prove a necessary accompaniment to the evolution of capitalist social organization. No wonder, then, that it was African religions—with their emphasis on the divinity of the apparent and the obligations of god to man—that provided the first vehicle through which the viability and utility of African cultures were to be denied; when the re-sistance to Christianity threatened to demonstrate the via-bility of these religious structures, cosmological failures were converted to moral failures.

Unlike the white presence in Mesoamerica, the early white experience in Africa was much more a process of inventing rather than obtaining knowledge. Partly, this was because the early "ethnographers" were often sick and drunk and had no desire to be in Africa in the first place. It was not until the nineteenth century that Europeans penetrated the African interior in any systematic or substantial fashion. After having destroyed the coastal cities, disrupted trading patterns previously intact for centuries, and irrevocably al-tered a delicately balanced yet highly extensive network of intercultural relations, it is little wonder that Europeans found indigenous people to behave as if in a frozen state of devel-opment. Despite the fact that coastal people were removed from their homelands and experienced massive cultural re-gression, some undefined capacity in their possession con-tinued to stir fear in white consciousness.

What is striking about the early periods of Western contact with blacks, according to Saunders (1978), are the periods of disappearance and submergence of explicit dis-course regarding blacks. From the end of antiquity to the ninth century there is hardly any mention or revision of the basic Ethiopian myth and, from the tenth to twelfth century, only slight revisions of the basic theme. Even for the Iberi-ans, who had the earliest and most prolonged interaction with African peoples, the issue of Africanity in any of its aspects—e.g., color, religion, history—is hardly deliberated to any discernable extent between the sixteenth and eighteenth centuries. Not only do these prolonged silences indicate a basic repression in the thinking about the black Other beyond heavily mystified parameters, but it also reflects the adamanty of Europe to be no more than it thought itself to be. This stasis reflects a potentially troubling recognition of inadequacy, a desire to exceed the predominant cultural definitions of self and society. For the European, the African became an ever-present repudiation of civilization—a civilization Western peoples, in many respects, wanted to repudiate but found that they could not do without. It may be that the African was viewed with the same ambivalence that thirteenth- and fourteenth-century notions of wildness produced—where the wild man was both good and evil, envied and feared, a superman and subhuman simultaneously. (These notions are, in some ways, not that different from contemporary perspectives of Africa as both traditional and modern, backward and advanced). As the European economy became increasingly dependent on African resources, such an ambivalence had to be resolved.

In seventeenth-century Europe, technological innovation and new scientific paradigms had been expected to confirm prior ideological traditions, serve old values and the wisdom of the Lord. That such novelty could not be contained within these traditional rubrics threatened to give rise to a new generation of paganism. It also alerted learned men to the extent to which the epistemologies of and fascination for ancient Greece and Rome continued to dominate contemporary sensibilities. If a traditional Christian ethos was to be maintained, a break from the predominance of

43

ancient textuality was needed. In order to accomplish this rupture and, simultaneously, defuse the forcefulness and potential threat of the new worlds opened up in Africa and the Americas, the ancient and exotic native were linked to explain and account for each other (Ryan 1981). The strangeness and newness of the native was defused by rendering him and his thought and culture as something already familiar and intimate. The ancient was considered no longer applicable because, in actuality, his was a primitive culture, one completely dystonic for contemporary European realities.Therefore, an act of self-denial (the denial of Europe's own cultural heritage) becomes the vehicle through which the Other is denied. Ambivalance about the Other is resolved in the shadow of one's cultural death. As Lévi-Strauss (1976) says, "the barbarian is first of all the man who believes in barbarism" (330).

After the sixteenth century, almost all ethnographies of blackness are unilaterally hostile. Colonizer and colonized become equally repugnant to each other. Partly, this hostility reflects the substantial increase in the number of both enslaved and free blacks living in Europe and the fact that they had often become favorites of the ruling class because of their exotic value.

Elizabethan cultural values and norms of beauty come to be expressed precisely in terms of color (Wavin 1976). Blackness is viewed as "some natural infection" (Saunders 1978) whose etiology is to be found in the greed, insolence, and carnality of black ancestors. More significantly, blackness represented the physical and visible manifestations of an absence of real knowledge; the soul is like a dark face, and the dark face stems from the emptiness of the soul. There was no longer any need for Europe to feel anxious about alternative cosmologies or the presence of a wisdom inaccessible to it. To be black now meant to be without wisdom, to be an empty space ripe for the imposition of Western values of perfection or antipathy that the Black World had to either fulfill or deny, but rarely could ignore. Without a knowledge of its own, Africa was either to represent the epitome of Christian values or what happens to a people when there is a complete absence of those values.

Having dismissed the immanent appearance of contrasting and potentially countervailing epistemologies, the European could finally settle down into his desire to know and understand what made the African tick, now that the cultural productions of the African did not represent a coherent worldview but were simply a series of discontinuous pulses infused with a child-like curiosity that could be shaped by a rigorous Christian education.

❀ 11 ❀

QUICKLY, HOWEVER, THE UNCERTAINTY REGARDING BLACKness returns to haunt the European in the form of sexuality. Depictions of unrestrained lust and mammoth organs spill throughout the imagination. Despite the fact that the majority of areas traversed by Europeans in West Africa valued modesty and sexual decorum, ethnographies vibrated with an often fond appreciation for the easy acquisition of sexual favors from the women, and coiled in terror at the monstrous dimensions of black penises, wondering what vagina could possibly exist to accomodate them (Saunders 1978, Wavin 1976). Much of the anti-slavery sentiment in seventeenth- and eighteenth-century England was actually anti-black sentiment fueled by the prolific celebrations of black sexuality articulated by the planter class in the West Indies. This made for a strange set of alliances, where racists and non-racists were temporarily joined on both sides of the question of slavery.

Fanon (1965) argues that no proper understanding of racism can exist without understanding sex or, I would add, the sexual imagination. In his early work, Fanon viewed negrophobia as the receptacle and form of a repressed anger at the enforced sublimation of white sexual and aggressive drives, the price of the white's denial of his own instinctual life for the advancement of the civilizing process. Kovel (1970) views the incipient forms of modern white racism as originating in the desexualization of territory, where slavery embodies the mechanism through which space is tamed and controlled, drained of emotional investment, and deprived of symbolic meaning so that it can be given up in exchange. Similarly, sexuality is to become contractual, an exchange of favors where sexual pleasure enters the cash nexus. If human beings can be converted into a commodity, so can any object or aspect of the body. The difficulty with this system of conversion and exchange for the white man is that it opens up a space for white women to employ their sexuality as a form of self-aggrandizement and social power. Therefore, the white woman must be de-

sexualized, made sacred and exclusive. The de-sexualization of the white woman drove many white men into the
chained arms of black slaves, initiating another round of
self-denial as the offspring of these encounters, themselves,
were usually enslaved (Williamson 1984). The black man,
supposedly unencumbered with the apparatuses of sexual
repression, must be denied and controlled for fear that his
overwhelming sexual drives will dissuade the white woman
from her commitment to being underwhelmed. Once the
de-sexualization of the white woman is institutionalized,
Kovel continues, racism becomes the vehicle for the resolution of incestuous desires and fears, as well as the form of
guilt for experiencing such desires and fears.

Needless to say, sexuality is a fundamental aspect
of all human endeavors and plays a predominant role in the
organization and experience of individual and social life. I
believe, however, that its importance in relation to issues of
race is primarily that of a "master metaphor." If sexual
fears and desires are at the core of racial exploitation and
cognition, something else of equal importance is also at
work. Additionally, I find it difficult to believe that incest
presently constitutes the limit of the imagination, the great
beyond.

In fearing black sexuality, the Elizabethan imagination signals its opting for the consolidation rather than the
transformation of its previous cultural efforts. There is a
move toward normalisation. The expansion of borders, the
formation of empire, and the extension of home base is not,
in the end, a challenge to the basic concepts of borders or
the sense of home. The issue becomes how to achieve sta-

sis. The doubt of white sexual potency is the doubt of white socio-cultural power, the doubt that the sacrifices made could produce the earthly and heavenly goods promised. Despite all the scientific achievements of the sixteenth and seventeenth centuries, whites had consciously diminished their belief in their sexual and social powers in order to adhere to proclamations of divine predominance. The social order was indebted to His wisdom and grace, and He, in turn, had opened up His kingdom to the meek and the poor. Before His sight, man always felt the debilitating strains of a bad conscience, and he toiled long hours to experience relief from this badness.

When faced with a people that did not devote the entirety of their lives to labor and who were equipped with the instruments of sexual potency, the white man actually faced the prospect of a people who could give birth to a "larger" society, a wealth of knowledge, a feeling of stature and self-confidence, a unity of spirit, and a stance of relaxation and comfort in face of divinities that white man and white culture could not match.

Through the vehicle of sexual omnipotence, we are thrown back to the basic anxieties Western culture experienced in its preoccupations with Prester John: Out of the desert (out of the most inadvantageous conditions) great and exemplary kingdoms could emerge. In Africa there existed a generative capacity to erect kingdoms from the heat Europeans could not bear. Alongside the rivers and in habitat that ravaged the white body with disease, there could be found a resiliency of behaviors and attitudes in people who did not fear the immanence of a harsh and final Judgement.

❖ 12 ❖

SEXUALITY CONTINUES TO BE A VEHICLE THROUGH WHICH THE intense and often virulent passions regarding race are expressed. But whether racial anxieties have anything to do with sexual experience per se is an open question. What sex is and what it influences become increasingly vague, begin to lose explanatory power. During the past twenty-five years, sex has been rapidly generalized into all areas of everyday life. Sex is about everything. Sex is to be that for which one lives, does in every kind of way, exhibits in every kind of text. Individuals have been encouraged to consume and consumate their sexual freedom. Where sex was once the unspeakable, it is now talked about incessantly. There are no more prohibitions or transgressions, except when it comes to interracial sex or the fear of disease, such as AIDS. Perhaps sex "saves" race, or race "saves" sex. These questions are difficult to answer because there is so much knowledge about sex that the individual doesn't really know what it is anymore, or rather, she can apply its name everywhere.

The absence of interracial sexuality from the various media, the maintenance of low rates of interracial marriage, and the passions which interracial sex still generates in both whites and blacks (albeit for often very different reasons) continue to siultaneously mask and provide the means of articulation for white fears that blacks possess a capacity for the creation of a knowledge ultimately transformative of how whites will be able to recognize and un-

derstand themselves. Even the origin of the word 'misceg-
nation'—a transform of the Greek word elaleukatio, meaning "from black to white"—provides a clue of the depth of
this anxiety that exceeds strict reference to sexuality. The
word was first used in an anonymous pamphlet that appeared in the United States in 1864, advocating that white
salvation rested in the negro, and that it was a matter of
utmost importance that Americans set aside their racist attitudes and marry someone of the black race in order to
produce an America of brown-skinned people (Aaron 1983).
The pamphlet turned out to be a joke authored by a promi-
nent journalist, David Croly, and was intended as a piece of
inverted propaganda in order to embarrass Abraham Lin-
coln. That it was a joke, perhaps, reveals much more about
white attitudes than if it had been proferred in a serious
manner. Let me remind you of the words of Ali Malim
which opened this discussion: "Blacks have their blackness." Only when the significance of blackness to the white
mind is being denied, can the value and importance of that
blackness be admitted. The postmodern white chorus sings
on: "We have no choice but to have no choice." Even in the
mid- nineteenth century, the problem is that whites perceive that there is something, besides money, that needs to
be saved.

In attempting to explain the source of extreme emotions in racial attitudes, Stember (1976) states that their
source rests in the idea that the black man can achieve an
experience of sexual pleasure with the white woman that is
unobtainable for the white man. This is because the white
man does not have an equivalent experience or level of

conquest accessible to him. The difference is multidimensional First, the sexual attributes of white women are high precisely because the white face doesn't publicize or readily display them, whereas, for Stember, the black woman's face closely resembles the genitalia. Secondly, the reasonable expectation that the white woman and black man are of dissimilar social status, that such difference is recognized, and recognized as not being prohibitive of sex is, itself, an integral aspect of the black man's sexual pleasure. Stember sees the core of female sexuality as merely the wanting to be wanted. The more the woman is wanted, the more receptive the woman will be. The white man fears this receptivity because he knows that an open and straightforward articulation of his wanting entails the necessity of a willingness to share power with her. For the black man, there is no power to share, yet, because of this, he will want the white woman all the more. As the attractiveness of white women declines and black men find other vehicles for the elevation of their social and psychological status, the resentment of intimacies between white men and black women increases. Therefore, the application of Stember's argument is that white men seek out the black woman in order to mitigate and qualify the advances that black men have made in non-sexual realms, especially as the black woman becomes increasingly celebrated for her "mixing of hardness and humour," for the fact that she can work, raise a family, get educated, be artistic and fashionable with a grace unmatched by the white woman.

Although Stember tends to totalize male sexuality too narrowly in terms of conquest and defilement, and mistakenly concludes that a specific female sexuality is virtually non-existent, he raises many interesting questions concerning the scope of the sexual imagination and the imagination in general. Too often the focus in clinical psychology is on conceiving the individual as having done or thought something bad or forbidden. Through intrapsychic networks of complicity, collusion, mutual projection, and unilateral defense, the individual designs and struggles for a road to normalization. Although the notion of an imagination is implicit in these conceptions, it is usually de-emphasized. The imagination is an object to be dismissed, implicated, or controlled. The individual struggles not to, but, inevitably, cannot help imagining herself as incestual, bad, guilty, inferior, or superior. Little attention in the field is placed on what the person imagines positively, on what she would like to experience or become outside the vague incantations to self-actualization or self-development. The question becomes, are others turned into the "refused" because one cannot stand or tolerate them, or are these others turned into the "refused" because it is impossible or dangerous or beyond the imagination to "be" them oneself?

One asks of Stember, why can't the white man envision new heights or forms of his sexuality, new modalities of expression? Why can't he use his imagination? Does he imagine himself as already dead, and does this particular kind of imagination refuse to die? It is rare in our lives that the imagination is allowed to run its course, act as a dream that opens up onto other dreams, where the dreamer is passed along to a variety of outcomes instead of being abrupted and dismembered. Once I was walking with my cousin on the street and noticed her obvious chagrin at a passing inter-racial couple arm in arm. When she couldn't tell me any-thing more than, "it's nasty," I asked her if she could imag-ine the two in bed actually making love and having or-gasms. She asked me to stop talking about it and not pursue it any further. If only she could allow the scene to run its course, the love making would be over and not much of any real danger would have transpired.

The white man who desires the black woman may find in such a coupling an unparalleled experience for his imagination: to be both black and woman simultaneously. The same could be said for the white woman, black man, and black woman. It is this symbolic acquisition of "impos-sible" aspirations which poses the real danger. What is at-tractive in interracial sex is the possibility of regaining a capacity to create a flourishing imagination; an imagination which does not simply represent an array of repressed cul-tural materials, but actually imagines and surprises.

❖ 13 ❖

THE IMPLICATIONS OF SUCH AN IMAGINATION CAN BE FOUND in an often quoted passage from Minister Louis Farrakhan of the Nation of Islam: "The black man loved the white man more than the white man loved himself." Whites have assumed that blacks in the United States had no choice but to make attempts to affiliate with them. This is open to question, however, for even though suicide had not been a conceivable practice in black culture, one can still ask why, under such abjection, did not blacks take the same course as hundreds of thousands of Mesoamericans and Native Americans and die by their own or each other's hands rather than suffer such vicious domination. Farrakhan answers this question by saying that blacks always imagined something else beyond enslavement, that despite the massive amounts of evidence to the contrary, they imagined their collective lives as one day different. No matter that many blacks had resigned themselves to living the real life in another life-time. Yet, through love, blacks are willing to affiliate with this life and with whites, extend themselves to the white Other without making comprehension or understanding of this life or the whites who dominate it a prerequisite for interacting with them. One day things will be understood, will be clear. Without something to know for sure, there is no definitive loss, no definitive threat. It is this love that the white man has always found difficult to imagine.

Black and white sex has occurred ever since blacks and whites encountered each other. It is likely that such interracial sex has had a hand in progressively dislodging sexuality from the rigid compartmentalizations of the eighteenth and nineteenth centuries. The actual sexual encounters themselves have contributed little to the restructuration of racial relations and, in fact, gave rise to a series of collective defenses deployed to compensate for whatever other minglings and interpenetrations might be implied by such corporeal ones.

My affiliations with black women always provoke inquisitions from others. The questions are rarely articulated directly; but I see them on people's faces; I see them in the reluctance formerly close friends have in socializing with me as a member of a biracial couple; I see it in the ambiguous mixture of overprotectiveness and criticism directed to my wife by her black friends, family, and co-workers. Although blacks talk to each other about such couplings, it continues to be something whites are reluctant to talk about, or talk about only in a diffuse and abstract way. The silence that characterized the early discourses about black–white relations continue to blanket the present social terrain. This silence is related to what Barthes (1974) labels "naturalization strategies": modes of exhibiting experiences, social imagery and texts through which the impression is created that there is nothing to find out, nothing to say.

In their various manifestations, these naturalization strategies have characterized the means through which whites have presented blackness and black–white interactions to themselves. Cultural ethnographies in a range of media have often:

1. Constituted images of blackness where the blackness itself becomes such an intense and exclusive object of fascination that the observer never has to think about what is at work to make the image or event powerful;

2. Cultivated images and repressions of images concerning interracial coupling where it appears that the image itself is everything, is so all-encompassing that all messages constructed to address it are inadequate or frivolous;

3. Presented images of blackness that are dessicatory, that go right to white anxieties concerning emptiness and hollowness, that assault the desire and capacity to inter-

pret what is viewed or experienced; and,

4. Presented blackness as an unsolvable mystery which no amount of interpretive labor will be able to resolve, where understanding becomes an impossibility.

All of these strategies are deployed to disqualify, retard, and evaluate any efforts whites might make to understand the dilemmas of race, or to imagine that racial difference could be organized in a way that is nurturing for all "terms" of that difference. If Fabian (1984) and Tyler (1984) are correct in concluding that Western knowledge in general is equated with that which can be visualized, not only cognitively but in an idiographic and moral sense, then to what extent does a racial apparatus employing such naturalization strategies act to convince us that there is nothing more to know or imagine in these matters?

In his critique of the ethnographic enterprise, Fabian (1984) states that when we look upon the Other, it is as if she has always been there and will always be there in her present form; that the Other simply absorbs effects, adjusts to them, and emotes to them rather than creating different version of herself for them and/or for her (Goffman, 1976; Uya, 1982). What is imagined is an unfathomable distance, even though there may be actual or frequent contact. Again, the extent of the distance is basically a matter of choice. Slaves in antebellum America could easily absorb a large portion of the Eurocentric belief system because many of these beliefs fit easily into or could functionally substitute for traditional outlooks, and thus serve as a source of cultural reinforcement (Levine 1977).

Forms of indigenous African "slavery" reflect the willingness of African communities and kingdoms to absorb outside strangers as retainers and dependents. "Slavery" was just one of many mechanisms used for acquiring and absorbing the Other as a resource, accomplished through a fundamental disjunction of the connection between what a person is and what she does. Such incorporated outsiders were never relegated to a single, unambiguous status. Each "slave" society affected various degrees and forms of assimilation, which were partially contingent upon the strata in which the individual was enslaved. There was no necessary common bond linking "slaves" in these societies, no unilateral categorization of the Other—sometimes she was intimate, sometimes distant. "Freedom" from enslavement and its accompanying social marginality was neither conceptualized or achieved as a distancing or separation from the community, but rather operated through movement toward powerful attachments (with kin or patrons) and belonging. Traditional forms of manumission increased rather than decreased social marginality. Although there is great variation among African societies in the mechanisms of slave acquisition and disposition, what is common among them is their ability to make the Other an integral aspect of their cultural and psychological lives. "Slaves" were not viewed as inferior humans valued only for their muscle (Miers and Kopytoff, 1977).

When I ask my students to describe the basic difference between whites and blacks, the most-often-cited factor is the degree to which blacks are willing to extend themselves to the outside, incorporate new ideas and influences with a minimum of a priori judgement. Minister Neal Massoud of the Nation of Islam: "Our power has been our ability to extend ourselves to that which seem implausible, to that which makes little sense....We have extended ourselves to both the unseen and the visible, to the fruits of our labor and the graves we have dug for them."

It is vital to attribute distinct cultural backgrounds and world-views to the Other as long as it doesn't provide whites with an excuse to conclude that the Other, after all, has nothing really to do with them, where the differences are "intended for cognition alone" (Bourdieu, 1977: 96). Neither should the Other be viewed as the perfect embodiment of the significant human values in order to denigrate a culture's diminished articulation of them (Todorov, 1984). The Other should not be celebrated as an act of self-contempt, or "as a criticism of whatever society and peace of mind one group of men in society has purchased at the cost of the suffering of another" (White, 1979: 180). This latter attitude has too frequently characterized the level through which whites have extended themselves to blacks in America, in a continuation of the radical Christianity of Spanish Jesuits, and the noble savage mystique of Rosseau and its resultant anthropology. Nor should such cultural differences be recognized neutrally or appreciated while criticisms of a race or culture are levied through citing deficits in individual character or individual underdevelopment (Apostle et al., 1983).

Black—white sex is not the charged issue. Such sex can be easily explained away, e.g.: most black women who sleep with white men are after the money or because of a black male shortage; black men who sleep with white women are after defilement or prestige. Everyone gears up to diffuse its implications, "it don't mean nothing" or "pussy is pussy is pussy." The thing feared, the thing which cannot be explained away, the thing that must be naturalized as an impossibility is the existence of black—white love. For the most part, American society can handle interracial sexual encounters, dating, or sex for material gain. But it doesn't yet know what to do or how to think when a white person and black person love each other, and establish a commitment to each other, and a willingness to dispense with the familiar procedures of relationship maintenance, acknowledge and adapt to the difficulties aroused by their relationship. In work and other institutionalized interracial relationships of qualified intimacy, there is relief and distance accomplished through their non-sexual nature. In sexual relationships, it is possible simply to impute carnality, curiosity, rebellion, or an implicit hostility being expressed to the partners' own races. But in an ongoing love relationship, there is sexuality plus the love, and it is this undefined supplement that opens up the possibility that there is something about blackness which is being viewed as deeply and personally significant and applicable to the formation and growth of white life. It is a supplement that may never be known precisely, never understood.

Black—white sex can take place behind closed doors. Black—white love must eventually spill out into the open, must find itself under the scrutiny of public gaze and intimidation. I think of the many times I walk down the street with my black wife. Many remind us that we are doing something wrong, even though these judges can only guess at what it is we're doing. We must tell ourselves that even though they guess right, someday they'll get into trouble for making quick assumptions. Still, we too have to make quick assumptions: that the hostility of the Other is private, it won't spill out here, and we hope we are right even though we know we've been wrong in the past. One can understand the anger of the black man all one wants, but the understanding doesn't cushion the impact of the anger, won't save you from getting your ass kicked if one man decides to break on you for reasons that have nothing to do with you. You are asked to respect a man you don't know by not having a relationship with someone for reasons that compel him to demand this respect in the first place. You must often de-sexualize yourself in face of the seductions of other black women who, once they discover that you're already hooked up with a black woman, decide to pay you a lot of attention.

Inside the relationship there are many indeterminacies. At times, it is difficult to tell whether you are simply absorbing the insensitivities and manipulations of your partner or experience her as insensitive because you, yourself, are unable to make the necessary intercultural adjustments. Caution must be exerted so that the relationship does not internalize the outside hostility expressed to and about it. Actions and compromises often are made simply out of the guilt partners feel for having rendered the other's work, family, and/or social life problematic or tense. Guilt over being white and black as an impediment to a full appreciation of the other's behaviors, styles, and thinking must be confronted. There are conflicts over understanding what you really cannot understand or tolerate over keeping separate and distinct the partner as person and cultural representative while, at the same time, realizing that this is an artificial distinction.

White–black relations have been characterized by long periods of silence. But as the Fulani, Bambara, and Songhai see it, this silence is the ground, the condition for the possibility of speaking, and not the vehicle through which speaking is killed off. From this silence, Aimé Césaire writes, will come "words out of fresh blood, words that are spring tides and swine fevers and swamp fevers and lavas and bush fires, flames of flesh and flames of villages."

3

The Cultivation of
Racial Difference

❁ 14 ❁

IN THE PRECEDING DISCUSSION, I FOCUSED ON THE WAYS
WHITES were unable to acknowledge a basic sameness with
the Black World. I examined white difficulty in making
productive use of basic differences. I now wish to focus on
how an unconscious acknowledgement or fear of that sameness fuels a racial apparatus, and how this apparatus is used
to produce and affect increasingly wide, marked, and unac-

knowledged differences between white and black worlds through a terror of indifference, where discernable abuse is neither recognized or intended.

In his book comparing the function of race in the United States, South Africa, and Israel, Greenberg (1980) outlines the activities of a state racial apparatus that coheres and solidifies the interests of a dominating class, where labor control becomes a state function and racism a state ideology. Race relations become significant, not as "an amorphous, all-encompassing relationship between groups distinguished by physical characteristics, but as a series of specific class relations that vary by place and over time, and that change as a consequence of changing material conditions" (Greenberg, 1980: 406). Within the context of capitalist development within a single nation, the alteration of such material conditions may not proceed in a unilinear direction. Forces may be simultaneously at work to both undermine and develop an existing racial order. As Greenberg points out, throughout the nineteenth century an aspirant bourgeois hegemony, with an interest in legitimating the state under law and normalizing class conflict under the domain of civic duty, repeatedly failed to dissuade the state from pursuing racial policies. The state relented only after a prolonged series of intense struggles with blacks and/or the bourgeois classes.

The primary function of a racial apparatus, Greenberg argues, is to ensure the compliance of labor forces, limit the proletarianization of these forces, and mitigate worker solidarity during periods when the dominant economic interests and class actors are changing. For example:

the destruction of subsistence agriculture and the conversion of productive forces into manufacturing and industrialization; the conversion of the industrial sector into an information-based service economy—these are changes which exacerbate and amplify workers' insecurity about their economic well-being. Reich (1981), particularly, emphasizes the role that Jim Crow practices played in breaking up worker solidarity and alliances between white and black workers.

The operation of this racial apparatus is not simply to publicize, explain, or orchestrate responses to the threats blacks pose to the economic welfare of the white working classes. Neither is it simply used to invoke some commonly acknowledged or disdained racial difference. Rather, it acts directly on the black sector to engineer individual and social behaviors that can be cited as evidence for its *de jure* or *de facto* exclusion from mainstream economic and political life. For example, slavery constituted a classic double bind. Whites feared the capacity of blacks to rebel in ways potentially exceeding the capacity of whites to contain them. The restrictions posed upon black mobility were often so severe as to render any attempt at resistance or rebellion absurd. Whites, then, would have an occasion to display contempt for the powerlessness of blacks who didn't even try to rebel (Baker, 1983). The initially-acknowledged powerfulness of blacks is transformed into a representation of their intrinsic weakness.

At times, the dominant classes minimize the difference between themselves and a subordinate group in order to preserve the legitimacy of this difference at a time when the subordinate group takes steps to amplify it beyond acceptable levels. For example, black aspirations for unique institutions and educational or cultural pursuits are sometimes met by white invocations of a common humanity or national identity.

At other times, the distance is amplified by the dominant group (usually in the form of generating "scientific knowledge") in order to account for the same perceived distance, now being minimized by the subordinate group, in order to defend positive self-identity or minimize the relevance of the difference for future interclass competition. We currently see the interplay of these processes in the debate about the continuation of affirmative action policies.

The important notion to keep in mind is that racial identity simultaneously dramatizes, masks, explains, and justifies social differentiation (Berreman,1972). The racial apparatus exemplifies Euro-America's romance with the totality of presence—the "just one look and you see everything" approach to human understanding. This romance results, however, in a series of misconceived interpretive practices, wherein:

1. Black individuals are interchangeable with each other, none being able in their singularity to add or detract from the basic notions of blackness considered by Western culture; and,

2. Black individuals have no worth in their own terms but must be evaluated in reference to everyone else in the society.

A comprehensive understanding of the racial apparatus must relocate domestic phenomena into a global interpretive framework of uneven development (Rex, 1981; 1983). In such a framework, American blacks are caught in the position of being actors at both the center and the periphery, and this position is played off against itself. In other words, blacks have one foot in a multifaceted class struggle from the position of the global periphery, as well as a relationship with metropolitan class struggles. Pressure is exerted on them to commit themselves (their thinking, behavior, political activity, kin-ship organization, and economic foci) to either one realm or the other. To make such a choice is virtually impossible, since most blacks are viewed, regardless of origin, as members of a virtual Third-World, colonized group in this country, and then viewed as Americans in the Third World.

Such a schizophrenic position is particularly difficult for Caribbean immigrants in the U.S., who find themselves displacing American blacks in the lower economic sectors or assuming positions which American blacks have refused to fill because of a degrading wage base. This wage base, in a Third World perspective, is seen as wage advancement. When confronting the full force of American racism as their economic aspirations increase, torn by divided loyalties and sentiments to home and adopted country, and faced with the fact that an increasing number of political struggles, disputes, and agendas concerning the home country are waged in the United States, Caribbeans tend to compensate for any identity confusion by assuming either socially conservative attitudes or exaggerated revolutionary sentiments.

THIS DOMESTIC/GLOBAL SEGMENTATION OF BLACK IDENTITY also describes the position of black workers in the American labor market. Black workers are disproportionately located in the lower sectors of a segmented labor market. In a study of the differential allocation of white and black labor across both industrial sectors and work positions (where the differential treatment of groups in terms of overall rewards and credential evaluation and the impact of that differential distribution of racial groups and rewards across labor market divisions were analyzed), Kaufman (1983) concluded that there continued to be a substantial gap between white and black earnings. Additionally, Kaufman concluded that there are no foreseeable, clear-cut, or readily obtainable policy mechanisms, short of a complete restructuring of American economic life, that could substantially reduce the gap. Kaufman implicates all aspects of social life: the differences between where core-sector production is now located and where skilled black workers reside; the declining profitability of labor-intensive manufacturing; the increased foreign involvement in sectors with high concentrations of black workers; and the low differential rates of return for educational advancement. All combine to impede black economic empowerment. According to Kaufman, upgrading the skill level of of black workers would contribute less than half to a general elimination of black/white earning differentials. Access to the core sector means access to an increase in black gross earning, but also an increase in wage discrimination.

❦ 16 ❦

IN RECENT HISTORY, THE MOST SIGNIFICANT OPERATION OF THE American racial apparatus has been the cultivation of a black underclass that inhibits cross-sector mobility by individual blacks and maintains black communities as hostages to the economic interests of a corporate elite. This cultivation takes place on a number of different levels:

1. It maintains blacks in a frozen state of general economic development through a host of policies that are implemented for economic rather than racial reasons, but which consistently militate against black advancement;

2. It transforms black residential centers into highly implosive communities of terror, so as to exacerbate behavioral patterns that can be legitimately cited as impediments to full economic and social participatlon;

3. It fosters a climate where the attention paid to the development of family, educational, and community institutions is often interpreted as surveillance rather than nurturance; and,

4. It structures black class-advancement as precariously dependent on governmental intervention and race-related job positions.

Basically, black economic well-being has not changed since the 1950s (Fusfeld and Bates, 1984). The economic progress that did take place in the 1960s is attributable to factors that can no longer accomplish ongoing black advancement: the temporary halt of manufacturing-job losses in the Northeast; goverment facilitated penetration into the white-collar sectors; the movement of black females into the clerical market and government employment; and civil rights activism. All of the following factors have operated in concert to reverse the progress of the 1960s, and to paint a grim picture for any further black economic advances (Fusfeld and Bates, 1984):

¶ The geographical distribution of blacks does not, for the most part, correspond with where new economic opportunities are located;

¶ The percentage of blacks in the core sectors has not increased substantially in thirty years, while labor-market-participation rates among black male workers have declined;

¶ We have witnessed the demise of high-wage manufacturing jobs and their replacement by low-wage service industry employment;

¶ Work in the service industry is often not full-time, relegating employees to extended periods of unemployment;

¶ Forty percent of all black families with children under eighteen receive Aid to Dependent Children payments;

¶ There has been increased migration of blacks from low cost-of-living areas to high-cost areas;

¶ Few opportunities exist for job advancement in the clerical field;

¶ Job upgrading for whites is connected to layoffs for blacks;

¶ Rates of serious disease, criminality, and unemployment for black males continue to increase; and,

¶ Black crowding in the low-wage sector depresses wages, decreases work incentives, and produces employment histories deemed ineligible for work in the core sector. Blacks who do penetrate the core sector displace whites into the secondary sector, in turn elevating black unemployment rates.

Fusfeld and Bates describe a circular process of economic causation, where the crowding of blacks into low-wage occupations becomes both the cause and effect of ghettoization and racial antagonism, which in turn is both the cause and effect of labor-market crowding in the secondary sectors. Thus, "blacks move into the high-wage sector without significantly modifying the process by which the bulk of the black labor force is crowded into menial occupations." (Fusfeld and Bates, 1984: 186). As Bourdieu (1978) reminds us, once a system of mechanisms has been constituted capable of objectively ensuring the reproduction of the established order by its own motion, the dominant class has only to let the system they dominate take its own course in order to exercise domination.

❧ 17 ❧

A SIGNIFICANT NUMBER OF BLACK RESIDENTIAL AREAS BECOME receptacles into which societal indifference is poured. One third of all Black Americans live in fifteen central cities which are becoming progressively underdeveloped. Once these cities are successfully vanquished, a black mayor is usually installed. A severely weakened infrastructure, a lack of local initiative in the face of political powerlessness, and the shortage of available capital make growth difficult.

In the postmodern city, people become disconnected from their living spaces. The site of residence loses meaning for individuals as well as for the persons who "share" that residential territory. Now the individual resident obtains meaning from her position within a larger hierarchy of overlapping networks that exceed both the place of residence and the resident herself. This is the case for all but the poor underclass. This characterization of postmodern urbanity highlights, then, the experience of confinement frequently reported by inner-city, black-sector residents. Everyone else is moving all around, unnoticed and unscrutinized. The density and poverty of the inner city give rise to desperate acts, acts stretching and challenging the bonds of tolerance that residents seek to maintain as a means for personalizing the collective experience of entrapment and for ensuring a margin of safety from the probable incursions of others, both known and unknown. Lack of privacy and tentative personal/household boundaries, although on one level culturally familiar, are tolerated as the necessary price for maintaining social networks where people watch out for each other. At the same time, implicit agreements of non-intervention are made when things get out of hand. Great effort is expended in conceiving and maintaining spaces of laughter and play. People try to make the transitions between home and outside fluid so that the aggression generated in both places doesn't disrupt the viability of either one. The resources required to permit singular expressions of identity through building something new often find their only outlet in expressions of destruction or effacement. Those who struggle hard for normalization of domicile and routine confront intensified fears that their success has only been temporary and, thus, a self-fulfilling prophecy gets actualized. Children are instructed to see clearly and carefully all that is around them. At the same time, they are instructed not to notice anything. Material accomplishments must be hidden to head off requests from others for loans, but at the same time must be displayed to assure the person that she is not, just like everyone else, going nowhere. In the same corners of rooftops and hallways children are conceived and their fathers are shot. In many neighborhoods with store after boarded-up store, what is confronted daily is the trace of an absence; it is an absence that lives. No wonder that the drug dealerships occupying many of these vacancies connote a mystique of economic vibrancy. Drugs make an almost self-contained universe: everyone can experience them without prerequisite. Drugs provide, thus, an experience which can be talked about with authority by anyone. In a strange convolution, that which makes the individual lose control is seen as the only vehicle through which kids can exert some measure of control.

There are some urban neighborhoods where the police don't go, except in large numbers. On the other hand, there are invisible mobilizations of resources and people, indiscernable yet sinewy connecting networks that ensure the persistence of large clans, both actual and invented.

People show up at doors without warning, at exactly the right times, perhaps in compensation for the times people arrived home to find that someone unanticipated and unwelome had already been there. This is the sorrow: that there are awesome resources, creative inclinations, and soul-*fullness* at work in black communities which are experienced only as compensations, only as ways to keep the basics afloat in an environment where the accomplishment of these basics (a structure of economic and psychological support) is a major undertaking. The vast discrepancy between what is and what could be created with these resources is a form of terror.

Long forgotten is the fact that it was white violence that presented the primary threat to racial peace in American cities. But whites were rewarded and blacks punished through policies that consolidated urban ghettos which, in turn, created the danger in black neighborhoods. From1900-1950, Chicago was redesigned as two cities, one white, one black. All the unrealistic and exaggerated fears whites had of blacks were systematically produced as actualities through the conscious design and enforcement of black confinent (Hirsch, 1983). This confinement was accomplished through a number of factors:

¶ Housing rules regulating neighborhood composition, where a neighborhood was allowed to maintain a fixed racial balance;

¶ Community covenants, dictating to whom a house could be resold;

¶ The restriction of public-housing relocation sites;

¶ Racial occupancy quotas;

¶ Intensive centralization, in which large-scale housing developments were constructed in a few targeted areas of limited acreage;

¶ Proximity rules, where newly available housing was exclusively occupied by existing neighborhood residents (justified by the argument that family and community ties must be maintained);

¶ Compatible-environment clauses, that sought to preclude multi-residential units from neighborhoods of single-family residences;

¶ Institutional development, i.e., the use of hospital and university construction as a buffer between white and black communities;

¶ Urban redevelopment and renewal as mechanisms for government involvement in the design of racial policies (a move strongly encouraged by private business as a means of reattracting solvent populations to the central city and reinvigorating the city tax base);

¶ Slum prevention policies instituted after entire neighborhoods had been cleared of blacks and reserved for private development (Hirsch, 1983).

Unlike the Chicago, Detroit, St. Louis, and Harlem insurrections of the great migration period, the rebellions of the 1960s had no whites to fight; a distance and separation between white and black communities had been achieved.

Even with the publicity and the resources devoted to the plight of American central-city areas, public policy reflects only a partial and equivocal willingness to assist particular individuals or institutions residing in black sectors.

Rarely does policy address the structural relations needed to transform black economic well-being: the progressive drain of skilled human capital; the reliance upon entitlement programs to compensate for the substantial discrepancy between income flowing in and out of the black community; and the general situation of discrimination and economic conversion that increase population density. Just as colonialists turned the jungle and desert (places of normality for their indigenous inhabitants) into places of terror, mystery, apocalypse, and negative freedom, so do postmodern politicians, corporate interests, and policy-makers turn the black sectors into zones of surplus terror and debilitation, zones which whites enter or traverse only at their own risk.

Practices of sociality and interpersonal affiliation, once familiar and nurturing in other realms, once tools of desire and growth, become infringments, expediencies, defenses, and compensations. They become archaic methodologies no longer applicable to the "real" world (the corporate sector) which is only minutes away. The marginality will not be accepted forever.

When people are wounded, they must compensate for their wounds. Already distorted and twisted out of shape, people in the color zones often distort themselves further as the only way to mask the initial debilitation. When pride and dignity are diminished, the easy way for people to mitigate the loss is to exaggerate displays of pride to ridiculous extremes, to suggest that such pride is an anomaly in the first place. Fanon once suggested that under racism black culture becomes uninhabitable. The terror for many people

76

residing in American black sectors is that it is still fundamentally dangerous to be a self.

❧ 18 ❧

THE ATTEMPTS MADE TO IMPROVE BASIC HUMAN AND EDUCATIONAL services for the urban black sectors are often used to deny the existence of improper white motives. A typical response, from a white fifth-grade teacher is, "hell, these kids just don't want to respond no matter what we do for them." Forty percent of black youth in New York City don't finish high school, almost a third of black youths in New York will see the inside of some remedial or carceral institution by the time they're eighteen. "Don't these kids know what they're in for if they don't shape up?" remarks a New York City policeman.

Youth resistance is here defined as stupidity, ignorance. Institutional personnel, both white and black, in schools, youth diversion projects, community centers, child-welfare bureaus, and detention centers usually fail to see this resistance and thus exhibit attitudes which regard their wards, cases, and students as "stupid". This, in turn, prompts intensified resistance. A perception widely shared by the black underclass, and even by black middle-class adolescents, is that the institutions within which they participate attempt to control them for no good reason. It is the "no good reason" which is the key and often-neglected element of their perception. By implication, if the reason was good, clearly articulated, true and trustworthy, it would be no big problem to accede to that control.

There is no absence of culturally viable and respected vehicles through which black youth can get a positive message. Popular voices—Public Enemy, Boogie Down Productions, and Slick Rick—warn of the dangers of drugs and criminality, talk about the need to stay in school. I've been around kids smoking coke in the back hallway at ten in the morning talking about how they got to get it together to go to school. When I momentarily convince one of them to get his ass in the classroom, he insists upon picking up a can of Old English 800 before going. The black community is turgid with stories of waywardness and positive injunctions. Everyone is implicated, tries harder, but the show goes on. Even though they know that these acts of being "outside control" (an imaginary, not actual condition) will bring in the cop, the bureaucrat, the psychiatrist, the counselor, the probation officer, and the social worker, these controls are not persuasive for a large number of kids. Yet, it is thought that more police, bureaucrats, counselors, and the like will solve the problem.

Despite the fact that these kids know they may victimize themselves with pregnancies, drug use, truancy, educational difficulties, and criminal acts, all of which open up their lives to multiple interventions by the state, the ante is simply upped; the actions become more intense and "irrational". Having lost touch with a sense and flow of expected ongoingness, retaining the ability to conceive of themselves as different only in terms of that which is unwanted or in terms of a stardom that will happen accidentally or by fate, knowing they will only be punished for displaying an incipient, albeit provisional, form of daring and adamantine behavior, these kids construe the demands of their households, teachers, and society as intensifications of the confinements they are desperately trying to shake.

In the early-middle years of childhood—ages 6 to 8—what a child thinks about herself, her efficacy, hopes, and future development, are largely shaped by her sense of what the world thinks about her. With so many indications, both explicit and construed, that blackness is something problematic, potentially difficult and prohibitive of real personal and social fulfillment, the black child must work twice as hard to conceive herself and actualize that conception. From a very early age, in the American context, one's blackness is something that must always be taken in consideration. Black parents do tell their children, "You must work twice as hard because you are black." Seldom do black children refuse to mobilize the energy and concentration needed to accomplish this double effort. The problem is that a large portion of black children are called upon to make it within social conditions that white children would be hard-pressed to operate in. Additionally, whites don't have to mediate their efforts within the omnipresent shadow of a negatively relevant racial identity.

Kids are not dumb. They see what goes on around them. They know who white people are; they know who black people are. They've heard the complaints and stories, observed the slights and injustices, even if their only contact with whites is through the television or in impersonal institutional contacts like the school or welfare office. Try as they and their significant others might to ignore the impediments or to redefine the impediments as sources of strength, as powerful legacy, many kids conclude that the world just doesn't think all that much about their blackness. Now they are realizing that the world is becoming increasingly indifferent to it. More and more, white people treat blackness as if it means nothing. Yet, all the kid has to do is look around in order to determine that white society is not telling the truth. If white society is not lying, then these kids must conclude that something is fundamentally wrong with them as persons, regardless of whether they are black or white. As a result, they are buffetted about in a permanent state of ambiguity over whether it is their blackness which is relevant to their situation or their personhood.

The more black kids know about the world, the more they are inclined to reach the conclusion that the world is fundamentally indifferent to their existence. Some successfully ignore this knowledge, others see it as a challenge, and still others often break, go crazy, and do "irrational" things as the very means to elide or circumvent the recognition. The serious consequence of this awareness is that both the intelligent and the ill-conceived interventions into the lives of these kids are perceived not as vehicles to help them more functionally and creatively manage the course of their lives, but rather as acts of surveillance, methods of watching and controlling them. Having performed in a myriad of case conferences in every conceivable type of institutional setting, I unequivocally agree with these kids: most efforts are little more than surveillance and behavioral control. Kids are talked about rather than talked with; classrooms infantilize rather than promote collective self-respect, initiative, or responsibility; treatment regimens reward self-deprecation. My concern is that the adolescent's suspicions—now thoroughly institutionalized and pervasive throughout black urban sectors—become applied no matter what the program is, that any program will be seen as fundamentally and irrevocably suspect.

America now becomes more indifferent to the realities, aspirations, and dilemmas of black people. When the perception increases that, no matter what is done, nothing changes, nurturance risks being interpreted as surveillance. Nurturance becomes resisted. "Nobody but nobody will straighten us up," concludes a sixteen-year-old boy. Refused is the normalization which is the goal of all surveillance—to render the person's behavior predictable, and thus amenable to being manipulated. With this resistance, a separation of white and black worlds is maintained. When a kid concludes that she is being denied access to a reasonable life and diminished as a person, one of the few options available is to simply turn one's self into a menacing instrument, to provoke fear and anxiety in those who have gained a reasonable life, to remind these people that they will not be entirely safe.

It helps some of these kids that there are blacks who achieve a measure of individual success—they are convinced to hang in there, work hard, and be patient. But for others, stories of success only serve to intensify the arbitrariness of the denials, impediments, and exclusions. These successes are often levied against them as assaultive accusations, e.g., "You see, other people succeed in striving to make something of themselves, there's no reason to use your blackness as a cop-out." I would add that there is no good reason for the kid to have to be in a position of considering the negative aspects of her blackness in the first place. Today, a black youth is still primarily a black youth; the kids' emphasis is not misplaced. Kids are told not to be so materialistic. And the kids are right when they say, "Tell it to everyone else in this country first, then we'll think about it."

In no way am I trying to romanticize the position these kids are in. Black underclass youth can be as sleazy, deficient, arrogant, cut-throat, loving, defensive, trustworthy, dumb, smart, out of control, and docile as anyone else. I'm simply attempting to identify the specificity of their situation as a group. This situation substantially impacts upon the development of individual psychological resources.

Fanon emphasized that colonization—alienation of a people from its possibility of self-determination—is achieved by means of both violence and ruse. Black kids recognize that there is a trick being played against them when the society says that the days of racism are practically over. What these kids are probably unaware of, however, is the way even their own resistance and refusals are used by the dominant social order. Since much of the knowledge possessed by clinical psychology has been generated through surveillance and various modes of incarceration, the psychological fields are aware of the implications of surveillance and incarceration. They are also able to speak comprehensively about the etiologies and formations of aggression and violence, deviance and pathology. Yet, these understandings have not been successfully incorporated into carceral or therapeutic practices regarding these kids. In most ways, the prisons and detention centers—of which the kids generally are no longer afraid—structurally replicate the very contexts which produced their aggression and recalcitrance in the first place. One cannot help wondering whether a class of kids is being intentionally cultivated to become the very menacing instruments that urban societies around the world are so afraid of. Foucault (1980) speculates that advanced capitalism requires the existence of activities which result in an unmonitored and untaxed cash nexus, i.e., crime. Marazzi (1979) discusses the roles criminality and an underground economy play in attenuating the economic and social demands of the lower classes: by providing static forms of employment capable of absorbing new participation, itself implicitly regulated through various modes of incarceration, dismantling of illegal enterprises, or attrition through death or incapacitation.

In an era where the general level of self-confidence wavers, the risk of attack in the urban environment tends to buttress and inflate feelings of self-importance, as well as enforce the limited use of public space. What I am saying is that the threat of crime may contribute to the renewal of urban individual egos. After being the victim of a crime, the individual goes through an initial period of "Why me?" where the arbitrariness of the victimage is resented, and which produces doubts in the individual's belief that she can protect the integrity of her selfhood. But these initial reservations give way to feelings of self-importance, i.e., "if I was attacked, I must be someone of some significance, picked on because I have something that others don't have." Within a group of those who have been mugged, individuals who haven't are frequently objects of derision and belittlement. Collective victimage becomes a rare, and thus valued, form of collective identification, a respite from urban anonymity, and a prerequisite for belonging to one of the few forms of urban communalism left.

Far from being a mere compensation, the road to self-aggrandizement through victimage may largely motivate the readiness to define teenagers of color as a growing danger. Additionally, when people feel threatened, they are willing to tolerate an increased expenditure of resources for more sophisticated surveillance technologies and activities, are willing to permit intensified incursions by the state into the personal details of everyday life. Yearly, there are proposals made to the New York City Board of Education to conduct ex-tensive psychological testing of pre-school children in order to identify a target population that is at risk for the eventual display of criminal behavior. These kids would then be watched closely for the duration of their school careers. Some have argued that given this expectation of criminal behavior, such special monitoring would actually increase and perhaps ensure the likelihood of its occurrence. Perhaps, this is exactly what the dominant social interests want. The adolescence of individuals of color becomes a trial balloon, a posse sent ahead to scout uncharted social and psychological domains. The posse may be killed, maimed, or wounded so that the rest of the society can occupy the social terrain that has been scouted with relative personal safety, without our looking as if we have debilitated ourselves to the extent our posses have. These kids pose the limit, embodying both what American culture aims for and what the culture must not become. In the same way that the deaths of real cowboys, outlaws, adventurers, and soldiers made images of these figures safe for general consumption, elements of the "street kid" figure are becoming incorporated into the general American character.

The adolescence of these kids has become an experiment, one in which the kids' behavior represents what is both wanted and unwanted, allowing the rest of us to increase our meanness, competitiveness, pathology, violence, and materialism—at least so long as we fall short, and neither match nor exceed the distortions of psyche and social being the society has cultivated in these kids. A reasonable life does not belong to most black kids, and even their resistance to this condition doesn't belong to them. No wonder contemporary urban life produces an incessant and hypervisible sensitivity in these kids, which is "kept on the surface of the skin like an open sore" (Fanon, 1968).

❀ 19 ❀

MUCH HAS BEEN MADE OF THE SWELLING BLACK MIDDLE CLASS. Freeman (1976), Sowell (1981), and Wilson (1978) rushed to announce that its growing numbers indicated the demise of race as a significant factor in the organization of socioeconomic life. As Pettigrew (1981) indicates, there have been substantial gains, and a general permeation of blacks into all sectors of American life. Yet this advancement is perceived as equivocable by the black middle class itself. Although its social mores become indistinguishable from its white counterparts, the uncertainty regarding the solidity of its status is reflected in its continued tendency to vote black, as almost unilateral support for the candidacy of Jesse Jackson in the 1984 and 1988 presidential primaries demonstrated. On a few significant political and social attitudinal indicators, the black middle class may be more black-identified than the black lower class (Pettigrew, 1981).

A large portion of the black middle class has been constituted through government employment. The continuation of this employment necessitates a politically mediated labor market, as opposed to an unregulated free market in the private sector (Collins, 1983). Rates of absorption and career advancement are contingent upon prevailing political sentiments, and are subject to fluctuations having little to do with the economic viability of these positions. Within the public sector, a majority of black positions involve managing the government programs most widely associated with blacks by virtue of their lesser incomes, e.g., aid to dependent children (ADC), public housing, health and hospital care, human services. Despite what former U.S. Civil Rights Commissioner Clarence Pendleton said about the wonders of black-owned private enterprise, the majority of these businesses continue to be oriented exclusively to black consumers, and have been unable to effectively penetrate white markets.

In her 1983 study of blacks in the Fortune 500 companies, Collins found 24 per cent of all black executives located in personnel departments specifically dealing, for example, with community action or civil rights organizations such as PUSH, which demand hiring concessions from these corporations. In other words, the success of these campaigns is often exactly measured in the number of people hired to make sure that these campaigns are no longer successful. Much of the advancement of the black middle class is dependent, then, on the continued attention and value the society in general places on improving the general conditions of black people. Diminution of this interest could substantially retard or even reverse the rates of economic progress achieved by blacks during the past two decades. Many blacks feel that the acceleration of black middle class growth during the seventies seemed to detract from the needs and the situation of blacks in general by diverting attention away from massive structural inequities that remain intact in all aspects of social and economic life. Additionally, this progress was obtained by whites assigning the direct administration and management of blacks to blacks themselves. By stratifying the black sector, the lingering operations of a racial apparatus are masked, and a widely accepted image can be produced that race is declining as a relevant issue—without the racialist organization of society itself being substantially altered.

The existence of a black middle class (or a "safe" blackness) fits in with the burgeoning ethos of the young urban professional, who wants to know just enough to feel that he knows just what is going on everywhere. The possession of diverse knowledges has become fashionable and necessary for rapid upward mobility. "I'd like to know everything that is happening, without going too far or doing too much to get it." That seems to express the prevalent attitude about cultural heterogeneity: an "I'd like to sample a little of everything" compromise. In an implosive design, the young urban professional is terrified by potential ignorance; she wants everything in sight, not in its *extensiveness, density,* or *concentration,* but in its sampled representativeness. Members of this class want just a little bit of everything, but not enough to start thinking that she has any alternatives in either modalities of thought or lifestyle. She must continue to be who she is. At the same time, the young urban professional wants to avoid the sense that who she is is a determination over which she has little choice. Once again, in the figure of the "yuppie," we return to the position where choice is denied through thinking that a choice has been made—a continuation of the basic psychology through which the viability, saliency, and contributions of the black Other are denied, qualified, or warded-off.

Many of my "yuppie" associates express profound appreciation for the fact that they are finding more blacks at the dance clubs and parties they frequent. "It makes us feel better about what we're doing," one woman confided, "that we all just want the same things out of life." One frequent visitor at New York City's popular club The World says, "I don't care who comes here, just as long as they don't take over the place." Yet many of these same people are unwilling to accept invitations to large family gatherings where there may be too many of the people "we just don't know how to talk to" or to sit down to dinner with my "ghetto bitches" (as one associate defines my black women friends from Brooklyn). "Listen, nobody is on a crusade any more," responds one man to the absence of significant black contact in his life, as if the volitional attempt to supplement one's personal network of relations with black interchanges becomes or necessitates a crusade.

A black middle class provides a representative and safe sample of blackness for white consumption. It assures whites that the significance of race is not really about race, but rather individual effort and determination— blacks want what whites want. If blacks are doing it—assuming a cut-throat, competitive spirit and careerist orientation, then the white young urban professional doesn't feel so bad about evoking those orientations for herself; she doesn't have to waste time with guilty attitudes or uncertainties that encumber her own efforts to get ahead. Instead of dismissing the experiences and conditions of the majority of this country's blacks through direct exclusion or discursive assault, the dismissal can take place through the vehicle of blacks themselves—"if more are making it all the time, then there's no reason that the others can't make it too."

IF GREENBERG'S 1980 ANALYSIS OF THE FUNCTION OF A RA-cial apparatus is correct—a means of minimizing class antagonisms, proletarianization, and worker resistance to new productive forms during periods of marked economic transition—it is reasonable to conclude that contemporary conditions are ripe for an intensification of racialist operations. America's economic base is now shifting to the production of information, services, and interest-producing capital. Such a shift necessitates a general reduction in the quantity of socially necessary labor. Moreover, it intensifies the competitive split in an already highly segmented labor market when the majority of high-wage manufacturing jobs are converted into low-wage service employment. The heightened competition for low-wage labor and the decrease in high-wage labor's ability to exclude a low-wage labor pool from the market are central factors in the intensification of ethnic subordination (Turner and Singleton, 1978). Presently, many companies are instituting two-tiered wage levels as a non-negotiable condition for maintaining currently employed workers at present wage levels, or for negotiating wage deceleration as the only means to maintain jobs.

If the conditions are structurally ripe for the intensification of the racial apparatus, does this necessarily mean new manifestations of the overt and virulent patterns with which American history is filled? There is good reason to doubt that previous forms will be redeployed, and equally good cause to doubt that there has been a significant diminution of racialist operations during the past two decades. The configuration and degree of visibility appear to be the only aspects of that apparatus which have altered. And there is nothing new about the silence.

As recent studies of white racism point out, there is little use conducting social surveys on racial prejudice (Apostle *et al.,* 1983; Banton, 1983; Pettigrew, 1982; Wellman, 1977). To the respondents of such surveys, racism simply does not occur much any more. The rejection is not of blacks *per se* but of their lacks, of social not racial deficiencies, and of individual rather than collective effort. That these lacks are institutionalized and not overcome by individual aspiration or compensation is not noticed. As long as black subjugation exists, there is an external reference to explain the lacks—it's just not an individual problem. But it is precisely this external reference that whites deny as applicable. In the denial of racism, racialist operations continue, becoming more complex by forcing blacks to constantly negotiate a disjunctive position where, on the one hand, they are criticized by whites for thinking that race is still a significant factor affecting levels of socioeconomic achievement and, on the other, they are criticized for moving too quickly into a full range of political, cultural, and economic domains.

Since slavery, most blacks have been convinced that individual black freedom and progress is not really possible unless all aspects of subjugation are unmoored from an association with blackness (Webber, 1978; DuBois, 1903). But it is precisely this overall upheaval and restructuration of American society which whites adamantly refuse to consider. Whites are willing to respond to blacks as individuals. (They are also inclined to explain black difficulties as a matter of individual insufficiency.) But whites do not focus on blacks as a collectivity. By accepting the collective elevation of black people, American cultural values of individualism and self-autonomy—often reluctantly suscribed to, and at a great price—are challenged (Gutman, 1976; Sennet, 1977). Once challenged, the absence of any cohesive or group identification based on whiteness means that there is a dearth of compensatory mechanisms available to whites to cushion and redefine a subsequent crisis in identity and self-value. Previously, individual instances of exclusion and prejudice were the vehicles through which most whites acknowledged racism. The broad-based acceptance of black individuals or subgroups into the mainstream now serves to obscure the continued existence of a racial order. People can now have positive images about black individuals, yet still retain negative images and ideas regarding blacks as a group (Synder, 1981).

❧ 21 ❧

ONCE UNCONSCIOUS, THE OPERATIONS OF A RACIAL APPARA-tus are free to spread throughout formerly unoccupiable spaces, interactions, and events. Implicit racism is more successful in getting blacks to shut up about their blackness. Currently, the racial apparatus seems to address the principle that "the breaking of dominance begins when the subordinate group reasserts its cultural or group identity" (Baker, 1983: 197), as was borne out during the civil rights movent of the 1960s. The nurtured fuzziness of racial difference is just one aspect of a general ambiguation of formerly crucial boundaries which articulated and organized antagonistic possibilities. Such differences now find themselves distributed in such a way as to negate or balance clearly us-versus-them positions. Additionally, it is precisely the openness of intergroup conflict that contributes to successful intergroup negotiations (Louche, 1982). The maintenance of a racial apparatus, then, may depend on its relative "silence."

The logic of postmodern cultural production appears to be the homogenization of difference through schizophrenia. Through a rampant production of differences (e.g., lifestyles, expression, knowledges, products, and consumables) the force of traditional differences in race, gender, and class

92

is vitiated. In postmodern American society, there is an excess of choice: 150 channel televisions, 150 different personal careers, 150 ways to have sex, 150 ways to leave your lover. Technology renders the copy indistinguishable from the original and, through the production of replicants, can disseminate the embodiment of any experience anywhere. The difference between here and there no longer proves significant. Mothers need their children to be both parental and dependent, chaste and seductive, grateful and frustrated. Home becomes the exile from work, work the exile from home, school the exile from the street, and the street the exile from school. Variations in real lives and outlooks become a multiplicity of codes, styles, fashions, signs, and signatures consumed and then discarded. Within such a climate of overproduced plurality, Baudrillard (1976) and Lyotard (1977 and 1984) conclude that the postmodern individual finds it increasingly difficult to produce differences of any significance, and subsequently difficult to imagine who he is. This situation is one of the reasons that, in the foreseeable future, whites may be forced to turn to blacks as the only group which continues to experience real difference. This move I believe is necessary but it is also important to keep in mind that it may, itself, constitute a dangerous rearticulation of the same racialist order that has maintained Western culture's reluctance to make such a move — i.e., instead of picking cotton for us, blacks will make *our* culture for us.

An additional means of avoiding racial distinctions is simply to acknowledge these distinctions in other guises. Race distinctions become cultural distinctions. When intersections on the cultural level prove too proximate, cross-fertilizing, or reducible, they become historical distinctions and then economic distinctions, class distinctions, regional distinctions, etc. These displacments become strategies for deferring a comprehensive confrontation with the basic differences between the experiences of whites and blacks in America.

Submerged, the racial apparatus becomes a nexus of inter-group collusion, where each group unconsciously uses the other as a repository for repudiated elements of their self-identity. Each group acculturates itself to and depends upon the maintenance of that apparatus as a means of self-preservation, even though that form of self-preservation is necessitated by the existence of that very same apparatus. Here, racism becomes the cure for racism. Sherwood (1980), in his psychodynamic study of British race relations, argues that the more the English attack Asians for their industry, the harder Asians work as a means of self-defense. The harder they work, the more the English hate them (since they see that their hatred has little influence or power to make Asians work less), and the less in touch Asians become with their impulsive life, which they must over-control. The Asians secretly come to hate the English because the English have the freedom to experience an impulsive life, and this becomes the means through which Asians keep an instinctual life alive, just as the English, through their envy of the Asians, keep alive their educational aspirations. Without the existence of mediating variables in these households and ethnic situations (i.e., family security, tolerance of mechanisms for expressing ambiguity, stress-coping mechanisms, efficacious family decision-making, resolved dependency needs and affectual interactions with caretakers) the racial apparatus threatens to become a necessary and permanent fixture of intrapsychic life. The racism articulated by one group is the compensation for the racism expressed by another group, itself fundamentally insecure about its own racial status. Pathology and cure interact in a viscious circle where it is difficult to get rid of one element for its elimination is perceived to be at the expense of the needed other.

RECENT RESEARCH IN SOCIAL PSYCHOLOGY SUGGESTS THAT classification and categorization themselves are important features of racial prejudice and stereotyping. Increasingly, such stereotypes employ multi-level conceptions in a half-hearted attempt to avoid broad generalizations. That is, stereotypes are made about the subgroups a person may belong to — e.g., the subgroups of women a particular woman represents: mother, bitch, executive-type, etc. — rather than general beliefs about womanhood as a whole (Hamilton, 1981). These subordinate categories become more indicative about actual discriminatory behavior. As the level of familiarity with blacks grows, the more stereotyping of blackness will occur on a subordinate level. Because individuals tend to overvalue the connection between infrequently concurrent events, and since it is negative behavior of blacks which whites most frequently hear about, whites often overestimate the frequency with which blacks actually perform negative behavior. This is why social movements which present "the general case" (i.e., present a large cross-section of the black community to white view) are effective in altering stereotyped conceptions (Snyder, 1981). The difficulty is that when whites act on stereotyped beliefs about black people, they often behave in ways that elicit the very behaviors misconstrued as typical. These beliefs also account for what is likely to be remembered and to unfold in the future.

Since judgements regarding human behavior are usually biased in the direction of expectancy-confirming relationships (Hamilton, 1976), even if blacks demonstrate one expected behavior and one unexpected behavior with the same frequency, white observers still tend to correlate the expected behavior with blacks over and above the unexpected. Information that dissuades people from stereotyping often simply remains imperceptible. People tend to scrutinize social scenes for evidence that confirms their thinking about a given situation, group, or individual; more importantly, people act as if these speculations already constituted the truth of the situation (Synder, 1981).

Rose (1981) emphasizes the importance of generating more information about interracial exchanges. This information, in turn, could be used by novices in such encounters to enlarge their imaginative capacities concerning what conceivable outcomes might look like. Rose notes a high discrepancy between verbal and non-verbal behavior in white interaction with blacks. While whites display a conscious willingness to accept and extend themselves when interacting with blacks, they often kinesically and unconsciously generate signals that are commonly interpreted by blacks as connoting self-consciousness, wariness, suspicion, caution, and defensiveness; of course, these signals inhibit or detract from the formation of intimate or even functional relationships. It's as if the white person is playing to an imaginary audience of judges who will discover a heretofore unacknowledged core of racial prejudice. The fear of coming off as prejudicial often leads to a reduction of white spontaneity and openness; it is precisely this which is interpreted by blacks as calculated and prejudiced. As one black person put it, "It often seems that whites have something to prove to themselves and nothing to say to me."

Once intimate relationships are achieved, shared personal norms specific to the relationship tend to replace group norms regulating and elaborating the contact. The problem is that as a racial apparatus acts in such clandestine fashion, the behavior and performance necessary for the formation of such intimacies are often undermined by the white individual's very desire to have them. The capacity for spontaneity, daring, and openness is gradually attenuated. The emphasis on ideologies of optimal and functional performance, infiltrating all aspects of social life, give rise to heightened, rather than diminished, self-consciousness. Increased black/white contact has vastly expanded white/black membership in the secondary and tertiary zones of each group's individual personal networks. But the primary zones — close friends, affiliates or intimates — have not yet been substantially altered, as might be anticipated from such contact.

Rose claims that "only when favorable outcomes are expected from a relationship will persons seek the experience and cultivation of the relationship" (1981: 286). Here one must ask, why don't more whites expect favorable outcomes? True, blacks as a whole are often wary of or hostile toward white people. Yet they have given whites the benefit of the doubt. A large portion of the supposed dislike is really a matter of cross-cultural misunderstanding, of miscues. For example, blacks tend to prioritize the expression of feeling (often very strong feeling) as a testament to the durability and resiliency of the other person. Whites tend to protect their status as Other through tact, assuming that people's sensibilities are fragile and must be protected from expressions of strong emotion (Kochman, 1981). Therefore, whites often see blacks as out of control, and blacks often see whites as rigid, controlling, and up-tight.

❧ 23 ❧

MY WHITE FRIENDS FREQUENTLY RESPOND CONCERNING THE relative absence of substantive black contacts in their life. "There's just too much baggage to get through." "Life is difficult enough just dealing with white people, and I don't have the strength or smarts to add this on, too." "It's just impossible. Every time I try it never works out, or they end up wanting something from me." By far the most common expression is, "They'll never accept me for what I am; they'll never get beyond me as white or trying to play some role, and I'm tired of being rejected."

There are matters of trust, affirmation that one is worthy of attention, respect, and consideration. A person wants to think she has value and usefulness. But when the talk turns to self-acceptance, I'm not sure what the self is that desires acceptance. To me, the self has been a tawdry, undefinable and volatile notion, difficult to pin down, let alone accept as a well-structured, and coherent package. Much of the sentiment surrounding the need for acceptance, I believe, stems from the progressive disjunction of the self as a subjective entity from notions of personhood as a culturally defined configuration. Additionally, the self has become a vehicle through which an attempt is made to define the individual as more than an administrative or social category — an attempt to ensure that the full comprehension of the individual exceeds that which is known and codified. If this is the case, it seems that self-acceptance would undermine the very reason why a concept of self is significant, i.e., as something incessantly resilient and malleable, without identifiable or coherent shape or summary.

Often it appears that what people want is no more than the recognition of their social competence and individual worthiness, or the non-recognition of their fallability, conventionality, or neurosis. Imploring others to "take all of me" doesn't make sense when most of us rarely like or even tolerate the entirety of our thoughts and actions. I often observe whites who tend to rush things with blacks, expect substantive relationships to develop quickly simply because it is an interracial exchange. If whites don't see trust and affection immediately forthcoming, they back off, claiming that they haven't been accepted. They often feel that if a sense of intimacy can be achieved, there will be no need to deal with racial issues. Given the history of race in this country, it seems unrealistic for whites to expect this immediacy.

As social cognitive psychologists know from studies of early childhood friendships and popularity, the fear of being rejected by others often leads individuals to act in ways which ensure rejection. If whites expect to be rejected by blacks, there is a strong likelihood that they will be. Much of the hesitation in white initiative, I believe, derives from the white sense that blacks know them more than they know blacks and, therefore, must face a basic inequality of power in negotiating the rights, practices, limits, and obligations of relationships. Common sense dictates that this basic perception may be accurate: Black survival has necessitated that blacks know as much as they can about white people. The limitations and inaccuracies entailed in this knowledge derive from the circumscription of black/white contact, and not because blacks weren't paying attention. White survival clearly had once been contingent upon using blacks; the successful exploitation of blacks meant limiting what would be known about them. The fallacy in using knowledge differentials as a rationale for whites to avoid black contact should be obvious: rarely do people enter into relationships of any kind with either equivalent knowledge or power. Rather, as Williamson (1984) elaborates, black identity today, and black development throughout the middle part of the twentieth century, has been based on a fundamental reconciliation of Eurocentric and Africentric orientations. Blacks have not merely assimilated white culture but have synthesized, reworked and reframed it, reinterpreted it through African orientations which have been preserved, revised, and transformed in the Americas.

What whites fear then, I believe, is neither the absence of acceptance or the immanence of rejection, but the recognition that whiteness is being known through interpretive frameworks heretofore unavailable to them. Whites fear that blacks possess a knowledge of whiteness that "exceeds" that of whites. It is strange that, within the context of actual or immanent interracial interaction, blacks go from being the people supposedly dispossessed of an identity to those who are the only ones who really have one. What whites confront is their sense that blacks have a head start in the basic knowledge of interraciality, a familiarity that enables them to dictate the terms of any relationship that depends upon something other than condescension or the manipulation of black insecurity. This situation may be homologous to the trepidations and reservations blacks have traditionally experienced in their dealings with whites. As the white person confronts the apparent Other, she has no priviledge of similarity or difference. Rather, similarity and difference are mixed, and any clarity may be mistakenly presumed. Consensus may undermine the relationship; antagonism may solidify it; and perhaps the inverse will be true. Whether or not the black interactant has more power in negotiating the interchange, most whites will conclude that she has.

This attitude borders on the revival of ressentiment, where white weaknesses are affirmed for the purpose of distracting attention away from the strengths of blacks. These weaknesses are used to excuse whites from making any substantial commitment to ameliorating race relations on an interpersonal level. Unwilling to be known or seen through aspects of themselves they don't know and, for the moment can't control, whites tend to do everything possible to avoid substantative interracial contact.

Citing the need for self-acceptance or the avoidance of rejection implicitly relegates the Other to the position of antagonist. Yet, as Goffman (1974, 1981) reminds us, the distinction between enemy and friend, protagonist and antagonist, opposing sides and partners is murky and ambiguous. Establishing sides and oppositions guarantees that there will be some degree of mutual influence between sides; each side "borrows" some of the behavioral characteristics of the other. In being an "opposite," a person can't help incorporating aspects of the actions he tries so hard to keep away.

In Goffman's terms, the self is an instrument for producing or concealing information which enables the individual to negotiate and maneuver through her social environment under a minimum of scrutiny. The self is a vehicle for the successful management of appearances. The self attempts to regulate the nature of attention paid to it, and attempts to ensure continuous access to the information produced by the social performances of others. At the same time, the individual tries not to look as if she is scrutinizing these performances too closely (Goffman, 1969, 1974).

The white interactant must not appear to desire the relationship too much. Neither must her behavior or intentions be connoted as embodying an insufficient desire She must act "normal," that is, express a desire for the affiliation as she would that for a white person. The situation and the desire, however, remain extraordinary and unusual, so the white interactant is obliged to "nomalize" an "unnormal" situation. Additionally, the white interactant must not appear to be revising or altering her standard repertoire of behavioral strategies so as to accomodate the extraordinariness of the encounter or the blackness of the other interactant. On the other hand, in talking about what should be expected of the relationship and the procedures for its maintenance, most blacks will expect that the reality of their blackness will be taken into conscious consideration.

To avoid being interpreted as calculating or unnatural in her behavior, the white interactant must consciously act out a behavioral style which is, in essence, her own. She must simulate herself but, at the same time, act as if she is not doing this. For if the white interactant appears to be controlling her behavior, she opens herself up to the intensified scrutiny of the other interactant. This additional scrutiny is usually met with an attempt to exert greater self-control. Because interracial interactions outside the formal structures of institutions may be an unusual occurrence for both interactants, they must watch each other closely for signs and evidence that the "'extraordinariness" of the encounter is being reduced, as well as confirm that neither interactant is deviating too far from their "ordinary" ways of behaving—the latter being measured by the perceivable degrees of self-consciousness evident in either interactant's performance. Each interactant is implicitly aware of common-sense prescriptions warning that the most reliance-inspiring behavior is often that which is most advantageously fabricated. As a result, each interactant must act as if she is really unconcerned about what the other person thinks. A feigned autonomy becomes the guarantor of any mutuality.

Interactants in everyday social encounters pay unusual attention to the displays of the other person in order to detemine what they, themselves, should display. At the same time, they are obliged not to appear as if this cross-checking is taking place. Yet, this mutual assessment does occur. Much of the white interactant's conception of herself in interracial exchanges becomes synonymous with the conception she forms about what the black interactant thinks about her. Regardless of the "accuracy" of these conceptions, they are based on the behavior, speech and thinking of the black other who is "designing" what the white person does just as the black interactant"s performance is "designed" by the white other. What is produced is an infinite series of reflexions and interweavings that must be consciously denied if the integrity of the encounter is to be developed and maintained. Each must assume that the other has a mind and life of her own.

In the process of trying to be accepted by the black interactant and by adhering to the micro-interactional procedures likely to produce such acceptance, an unconscious diffusion of the black other's "knowledge" to the white interactant takes place. However, this "knowledge" or sensibility must be acknowledged all along as the white interactant's knowledge and sensibility. In the interracial interchange, blackness leaks into whiteness; whiteness leaks into blackness. The only problem is that in order for the interchange to preoceed smoothly, no one can explicitly acknowledge that this level of leakage is occuring. Nevertheless, this leakage is a countervailing process in regard to the distribution of racialist effects, an indiscernable counter-discourse to the malignancies of racial power. But as unconscious, this discourse remains unelaborated in terms of interactants knowing what it really affects. For all practical purposes, it takes place without taking place.

Although displaying concern for the integrity of personal identity may be necessary for the ongoingness of any social transaction, a preoccupation with the "authenticity" of an articulated individual identity may limit the elaboration and enjoyment of social experiences. To borrow a metaphor from Serres (1983), to be social, to be an "I" among other "I's" is like playing a game with a ball. The ball (i.e., the identity) is meaningless, is nothing by itself, but requires players who follow and serve the ball instead of making the ball follow them. The ball circulates, is passed, taken, and given up quickly. This circulation of the ball means that at different times and locations on the playing field (the social arena), different players are tackled, exposed, substituted, and paid attention to. A person exists to pass her identity around. The possibilities of sociality are limited by programmatic desires for fairness in interpersonal encounters, e.g., "be fair and accept what I have to offer, don't reject it;" "I keep the ball this long and then you get it, or let's divide the ball in two, or get two balls, and just play alone, or, better yet, let's just throw the balls away."

If whites are to participate in any substantial interracial social experience, they will have to take enormous risks. Deprived of a clear sense of success, fulfillment, or adequacy in these relationships, they will need to keep going beyond what they think is sufficient, beyond who they think they are as individual characters. What frightens me about

105

the behavior of many of my white friends is that they give up too easily, are too quick to list their fallibilities and to itemize the impossibilities of any "real" and comfortable interchange. Granted, the process will not be easy or even "real" in the existential sense that many whites value.

Rex (1983) describes racism as the idea that undesirable qualities are innate and immutable beyond the course of individual action, "where the practices of ascriptive allocation of rules and rights are justified in terms of some deterministic theory" (160). Postmodern America may have come to the point of propagating racism by inverting it. That is, it is precisely the acknowledged fallibilties, weaknesses, and uncertainties of whites thmselves, and their inability to do anything about them, which are claimed to preclude any extensive integration of white and black sectors. The message is: "It is because we are so fucked up ourselves that we are unable to do anything really significant in terms of altering racial realities." Instead of whites deprecating blacks, whites deprecate themselves, convince themselves that they don't have the psychological fortitude and resources necessary for the task of relating in a different way with black people.

❀ 24 ❀

AS I HAVE SUGGESTED THROUGHOUT THIS CHAPTER, THE postmodern racial apparatus is a highly mobile operation when "exiled" into the unconscious. There it limits both individual and social imagination and produces doubt in individuals about their efficacy. The mobility of this apparatus is partially dependent on a multiplicity of racial significations which generate many different forms of interracial accommodation, e.g., segregration, symbiosis, consociation, amalgamation, assimilation, differential incorporation (Kuper, 1981). The more confusing concepts of race become, the more race can be invoked to mean many different things, and thus spawn many different forms of social interchange.

With the existence of diffuse and multi-faceted racial statuses, what prompts racial conflict and forms of resolution may vary greatly. In the United States, race has been used as an instrument to disguise, reveal, articulate, mitigate, and accentuate the force, apprehension, and efficacy of social class as a unit of social categorization, antagonism, and change. Yet, even though race serves this function in relationship to social class, it also exceeds class considerations. Although provoked by shifting material conditions, specific states of race relations are not consistently matched or correlated with particular economic transformations (Blumer and Duster, 1981). There is no set pattern that dictates whether exclusion will follow periods of high unemployment or whether integration will proceed from periods of economic well-being.

4

On the Denial and Survival
of Black Offerings

❀ 25 ❀

ALTHOUGH MANY OF THE BLATANT TRAPPINGS OF RACISM ARE
gone, a seemingly impenetrable disjunction between white
and black life remains. Increasingly, blacks suspect that the
attenuation of these blatant trappings was necessary for the
resuscitation of a racial apparatus—the basic system remains unaltered.

Recently I witnessed an interchange on a bus where a white man and black man got into a small dispute over a seat. The white man opened the "dialogue" by saying, "Look it, man, we (are) all minorities on this bus." My concern with the white passenger's attitude is not so much that he denies the black access to a minority status by assuming it for himself. Rather, my concern is with the fact that the white man may really see himself as a minority, with limited, provisional, and basically uncertain connections to a larger social community whose values and ideals he supposedly represents. Accompanying this perceived absence of social connection and community membership is the probable decline in felt notions of social responsibility and interdependency, where a person's own well-being is inextricably linked to the well-being of others. It could be argued that such notions have been exclusively the ideological buttressing of capitalist irresponsibility; yet, these notions did play a key part in motoring the social transitions of the 1960s. They constituted the conscience to which many forms of black struggle were directed, i.e., the appeals to religious spirit and to American ideals of equality and freedom. I am afraid that there may not be much of a conscience left.

 26 ❧

THE PRIMARY FOCUS OF THIS DISCUSSION SO FAR HAS BEEN ON the white refusal to see something of relevance and value in black life, something that could be applicable to and nurturing of white psychological and cultural development.

Often when black contributions are used, whites deny the blackness of the origin. In previous sections I have dealt with the ways a white racial apparatus: (1) refuses to accord a position of similarity to the black world sufficient for valuing and utilizing the differences; and, (2) affects increasingly wide and marked differences between white and black worlds as a function of an unconscious fear of a basic similarity.

I now want to deal more explicitly with the rationales that have been used to diminish the applicability of black cultural productions to white lives. These rationales have been variegated and frequently contradictory. They have been articulated from both left and right on the political spectrum. At times, they have been unintentionally fueled by otherwise powerful political critiques of racism and colonialism by both whites and blacks. A sampling of such rationales would include the following.

1. There are no distinctly black cultural parameters or practices of signification in Black America before or after emancipation, or in Africa after the onset of both the colonial and neocolonial periods.

2. If there are distinctive cultural structures in postcolonial Africa, they have simply intensified the everyday crises of individual Africans; they inhibit their individual and collective development.

3. The only salient difference between white and black worlds is one produced solely by a legacy of domination and exploitation. Slavery and colonialism subjected the Black World to a period of cultural sclerosis, where indige-

nous cultural forms became inert, unusuable and, in many instances, pathological.

4. The cultural differences between white and black worlds are so marked that any reconciliation or white borrowing of black cultural precepts is impossible or merely contrived.

5. If there are distinct cultural parameters to the black American experience, they are basically insignificant in terms of the basic issues regarding socioeconomic survival. Additionally, there is nothing to connect these cultural formations to those of blacks in Africa or the Caribbean.

6. What appear to be cultural differences are reflections of differences in the intelligence, cognition, and sociality of basically similar peoples.

7. There may have once been a distinct African–American culture with linkages to Africa, but it doesn't exist anymore.

8. Even if blacks and whites have distinct worldviews, these views are an abstraction or retrospective rationalization of prior behaviors and have little structuring or predictive capacity.

9. The traditional thought which has characterized much of the Black World is fundamentally concrete and, thus, either insufficient or incoherent to Western cognition, because it is incapable of adjusting to contemporary environmental conditions. With the imposition of Western administrative and pedagogical structures during the colonial period, much of this thought has been vanquished anyway. The successful development of African productive capaci-

ties through technological transfer, the rebuilding of an agricultural infrastructure, etc. should be the primary focus of Western interest in Africa.

In this section I will attempt to discuss these rationales, with an eye not to their critical dismissal, but to their irrelevance as obstacles to the major point in question. Debates about cultural and epistemological distinctions will continue without resolution or the addition of supplementary substance in the foreseeable future. For much of the Black World, sheer survival is the sole preoccupation, as nations and economies fall apart or become mere appendages to Western economic interests. In the long run, it doesn't matter whether there exist discrete Black World philosophies, cultures, or understandings. Rather, it is the thoughts and experiences of blacks regarding philosophy, culture, and understanding which are important. This importance far outweighs considerations of whether these thoughts and experiences can be systematized or viewed as collective coherencies. The main task is getting whites to take the speech, actions, feelings, and thoughts of black people seriously and regard them as significant influences.

It is important to keep in mind that many thoughts and propositions are independent of the place of enunciation. Others are directly and exclusively applicable to that place, and still others are able to convert, reframe, and alter the place itself (Wright,1979). There is no sense here that the efficacy of such thoughts and propositions are necessarily contingent upon a form of systematization one might designate as culture.

That said, I do believe that an African orientation has persisted, through direct inclusion and reformulation, in Black American practices of signification. Africanity is an ongoing process of cultural invention, motivated by the continuously shifting status and activist positions assumed by blacks in America (Abrahams, 1970; Clark, et al., 1975; Hannerz, 1968, 1972, 1975; Hoetink, 1973; Jackson, 1980; Mintz and Price, 1976; Nobles, 1974, 1980; Pescatello, 1972; White, et al., 1980).

Wade Nobles (1980), who has pursued this issue perhaps more than any oher contemporary academic, claims:

> To determine whether and to what extent the African orientation has persisted, one must ask, "how could it have been maintained?", "what mechanisms or circumstances allowed it to be maintained?" An orientation stemming from a particular indigenous African philosophy could only be maintained when its carriers were isolated (and/or insulated) from alien cultural interactions andif their behavioral expressions of the orientation did not openly conflict with the cultural-behavioral elements of the "host" society. If the circumstances of the transplantation of New World Blacks met one or both of these conditions, then it is highly likely that an African orientation was sustained. (327)

Similarly, Mudimbe (1983) argues that it is important to determine the present use of African references or mythic constructions in supporting current black American beliefs about cultural distinctiveness and reframing interpretive mechanisms used to evaluate black thinking and behavior—what Jones and Dzidzienyo (1976) call a "dynamic Africanity."

Instead of learning and applying a body of clearly and consensually defined Africanisms in the American context, black Americans, especially in the last thirty years, have increasingly sought to:

1. Africanize existing norms and practices, explicitly label and view an African character within a set of social practices;

2. Invent new forms of speech, references, and uses for ancestor invocation, self-contemplation and evaluation that are believed to reflect or possess an essential African spirit; and,

3. Redirect thresholds of tolerance, redefine notions of individual and social responsibility, and establish new modes of individual accountability in accordance with a perceived African ethos.

These practices are not the defense or memory of a pre-existing set of cultural practices but an active attempt to reconstitute a culture through constantly reinventing Africa.

❧ 26 ❧

CRUCIAL TO THIS DISCUSSION IS THE VIEW OF CULTURE AS something other than primarily a system of artefacts, propositions, rules, and beliefs, but as "associative chains and images that suggest what can be reasonably linked to what in a particular setting" Rosaldo, 1984: 140); where culture provides images suggesting particular ways to combine thoughts, feelings, and actions. The emphasis here is on cultures as methodologies for the constitution of self and society rather than as a series of heterogeneous representations of universal individual and social chracteristics, even though there may be aspects of universality in many human desires and functions.

Also emphasized here is the notion of world-view as an expression of a people's ontology, history, and values. Such world-views reflect the relationship of cultural norms to individual norms and posit the nature of personhood for a particular culture. Maruyama (1978) describes world-view as "the underlying structure of reasoning an individual exhibits as a member of culture, which may not necessarily be made explicit or visualized, but which manifests itself in various aspects of the life of the individual as a member of culture" (83).

World-views generate the cognitive and ideological presuppositions that individuals articulate in constructing the understandings and explanations of life experiences which are transmitted to various others. These understandings greatly affect how individuals interpret their position in the world. How individuals understand contemporary environmental, social, personal, and geo-political changes affect how they will respond to these changes, how they will identify themselves, account for their behavior, and construct frameworks for interpreting the behavior, policies, and thoughts of others and their institutions, what individuals will perceive as threats to their identity, who they will affiliate with, and what they will view as legitimate authority (Berry, 1976; Comaroff and Sim, 1981; Doob, 1971, 1975, 1983; Harris and Heelas, 1979; Shapiro, 1981; Witkin, 1978; Witkin and Berry, 1975).

World-views embedded in specific political cultures: (1) create accessible and legitimate courses of action and allowable alternatives, and; (2) constitute and cohere normative orientations, social practices, and individual behaviors (Ardener, 1971, 1981; Bailey, 1983; Duvinnaud, 1962; Geertz, 1973, 1983; Heelas and Lock, 1981; Leenhardt, 1979; Rosaldo, 1980; Shweder, 1980).

It is on this level of world-views that the significant disjunctions between white and black worlds can be found. It is also the appropriate framework for identifying linkages among various facets of the Black World. Sowande (1974) suggests that a number of elements on the level of world-view characterize basic similarities among various black cultural manifestations. These elements include the recognition of a suprasensible or invisible world of silence; life as the totality of being and of the manner in which the divine core of being and individuality as its manifestation act to polarize the other; the multiple-bodies of the individual and the form of their cohesion and dispersal.

Despite the fact that such world-views may not be capable of producing feasible strategies for negotiating postmodern everday life either in America or Africa, these views simply don't disappear. Rather, they are relegated discrete territories of operation and are compartmentalized away from the world of work and other institutional contexts (Binet, 1984).

A common assumption today is that a reduction in the psychological distance between distinct cultural regions and an increase in the speed of human movement tend to exert a strong homogenizing influence on cultural differences. Everyone comes to look like each other: the rich try to look poor; the poor try to look rich; the South consumes radios and movies with a voraciousness matched only by the North's tendency to celebrate refuse. The South gravitates toward "the good life"—the world knows where the action is, knows where the foci of the impacting forces are located. On to America. Faced with a substantial alteration of the national complexion, the influx of Asians, Africans, Latins, and Caribbeans, and confronted with the influx of invocations and habits they pretend to celebrate but don't really understand, today's whites rush to acquire a taste for the proclivities of the new browns and blacks. "We must make what they bring our own," is the rallying cry of the white urban. Even if the threads of Third World cultures are interwoven into the fabric of postmodern white culture, whites will go to great lengths to produce these threads themselves. In this way, whites do not have to deal with the complexities of the Third World producer's political and psychological situation, her aspirations, fears, memories, guilts, or histories.

Yet, there is much evidence that, in the context of accelerated global interdependence and the apparent homogenization of cultural productions, the elaboration of worldviews in the Black World does not necessarily move toward conformity with white, Western views, or does so only at different speeds within the internal population of a given society (Alverson, 1978; Amer and Isaacs, 1978; Jahoda, 1973, 1975; Johnson, 1981].

Ardener's (1981) distinction between pardigmatic and syntagmatic levels of cultural formation may help us understand the interconnected nature of cultural practices in the Black World. In his scheme, basic cultural knowledge and practice on the paradigmatic level is not readily codifiable, a kind of systematic and collective intuition that works through different types of specification which, in turn, affect how and when such knowledge and practices are used. In analyzing any cultural formation or event—expressive, symbolic, or ritualistic—the observer derives a level of meaning through being able to measure, count, locate, identify, and record participants, instruments, expressions, classifications, arenas, repetitions, incidents, ages, genders, etc. But the level of meaning that obtains from these syntagmatic pursuits is rarely adequate to the kind of comprehensions often instantaneously achieved by the participants themselves. In other words, despite the proficiency and exhaustiveness of the analysis, there are often means of knowing that exceed linguistic description.

For example, a family converges nightly upon a dinner that is primarily prepared the night before. The time at the table is regularly consumed with questions concerning the various activities in which the two children are engaged, the two parents alternating turns in the questioning. For the two hours following the meal, each family member retreats to an individually possessed space to complete various homeworks, regrouping for dessert two hours later. After a few minutes, the two children move to the next room and watch television while the couple awkwardly attempts difficult intimacies in conversation—attempts which the husband quickly vacates to assert authority over the selection of TV channels in the next room, which, in turn, prompts disagreement between the children over which show is desired. One of the children inevitably sides with the father's preference, which is calculated to correspond with the child whose turn it is to later help the mother prepare the next day's meal. The "legitimate" viewing turn is perpetually "out of sync" with the mother's assistant's turn. The slighted child provokes either a physical or verbal altercation with the other child, who exaggerates her disgust by withdrawing from the scene minutes before the mother enters the room to scold the remaining child and chastize the father for his complicity in permitting the altercation.

At this point, the father defends the child whom he "sided" against earlier, and the mother intensifies her criticisms of the child. The slighted child re-emerges from her room to instruct the parents to lower their voices. The father informs the child that she is out of line. The mother and child who she has been criticizing join together in mocking the father's inability to enforce discipline, which in turn becomes the father's cue to withdraw and fall asleep in his bedroom while the mother and child return to the kitchen to prepare for the following night's round. With some variations these conflicts and maneuvers—the basic configuration of shifting, yet adamantly static alliances and precluded exchanges—remains the same night after night.

An observer could attend to who does what to whom how often in specific temporal and spatial locales, charting the dynamics of mutual causality and feedback loops that amplify and counteract the behavioral alternatives accessible to each family member and the group as a whole. But these efforts are not adequate for determining how the family knows—so quickly, methodically, and thoroughly—what to do and how to respond in these nightly rituals.

The individual members "design" their behaviors through a matrix of images, equivalences, constraints, and propositions which generate an experience capable of producing an excess of interpretive activity. In attempting to account for why this family does what it does, the observer confronts the possibility that there may be many knowledges for sure, many discrete and often contradictory means of rendering the experience sensible, all or none of them being at work at different times; all of them speculations about whether or how the individual family members know what they are doing. Often it is not a case of people subscribing to or believing in particular justifications for their explanations/behaviors but, rather, simply believing in their potential justifiability, even if they act as if a clear justification is implied (Nunberg, 1981).

It is quite likely that this relational logic, where the need for shifting alliances between the marital couple and their children is connected to the foreclosure of any substantial intimacy between the couple, could produce vastly different behaviors and scenarios in different families. Even the realization of such intimacy could result in the overt or conscious cancellation of the relationship. In other words, if the couple were able to be intimate with each other, it is possible that the marriage would not last.

Another example of paradigmatic and syntagmatic analytical distinctions can be found in the study of contemporary healing cults. In assessing the accelerated proliferation of these cults in almost all Third World urban areas and Western cities with large Third World populations, it is important to evaluate the nature, use, and efficacy of each method separately. Some of these healing methods reflect a crude fascination with the parodied exaggerations of disembodied Western symbols and the magicalized war machines of postmodern imperialism. Others emanate more or less directly from the cosmologies that have been valued and used by a particular cultural region for centuries without interruption. Whether functional resistances or destructive complicities, each method may be motivated by an attempt at healing born from an implicit relationship between personal misfortune, a collective inability to reverse the increasing terror of material and psychological life, and the dissipation of indigenous cultural values and coping mechanisms once available to mediate the oppressions applied. Whether bogus or genuine, each is generated by a culture's need to simultaneously represent their powerlessness in the face of massive disruptions of familiar and valued life and an unwillingness to submit to this powerlessness. On a syntactic level, the methods may appear the same, may be unable to cure the specific disease at hand, but their effects on specific individuals and situations may be vastly different—"saving" unknown and unrecorded others as the "recorded" ones die.

Attempts at healing escalate when people feel they can exert little control over the course and outcome of life events. Always provisional, cure both fails and succeeds at cushioning the hardships. The failure rests in the fact that belief in the healing's efficacy intensifies the absence of self and collective control—part of the reason why such healing mechanisms are turned to in the first place.

Although the terms of the healing emanate from the individual's own faith and discipline, from her belief in the efficacy of the healer and her practices, the individual, herself, is not responsible, is not the author of the cure. In fact, she must usually reliquish all control in order for the healing to work.

When a people perceive that they're unable to volitionally influence the course of their lives with efficacy, authority, and legitimacy, external domination is pervasive and effective. This, in turn, intensifies feelings of impotence. No single knowledge of salvation, no single liberating knowledge successfully articulated and adhered to can ensure a radical disposition of collective outcomes. It is not that there is nothing for certain; there are just too many things for certain.

Whereas the specifications of paradigmatic structures may be vastly different in the distinct sectors of the Black World, this lack of surface consonance does not imply that referential values and inclinations are not shared. Additionally, Ardener (1981) continues, culture responds both to physical/environmental occurrences and the scanning of their reactions to these occurrences by persons and groups both indigenous and exogenous to the culture. A culture actively responds to the processes used to record how it operates. Whatever is produced by a culture already embodies the methods applied to understand it and reflects what others have to say about it. "Even the extraordinary complexity introduced into the (cultural) surface by the rapid transmission of provisional maps of its own configurations still does not utilize more than a fraction of the complexities of the individuals occupying it" (Ardener, 1981, 321).

The mediation of the relationship between what it does and what it thinks a "recording surface" registers about what it does often becomes the major preoccupation of culture. The importance of this point for our discussion is that, under the surveillance of colonial, plantation, and urban administrative gazes explicitly hostile to the development of black individual and cultural bodies, inordinate energy may have been expended by blacks simply to fight against intentions to erode and level them.

The attempt to deflect attention away from indigenous cultural productions becomes highly significant, a major aspect of cultural production itself. In the end, what the outside observer knows about these indigenous cultures are little indication of the generative capacities of black peoples. Rather, they are traces of the tensions between: (1) the attempted imposition of alien cultural forms, intensive surveillance, and circumscribed cultural mobility and expressive freedom and (2) black attempts to deflect these impositions, conceal cultural imperatives, regularize intercultural contact, and become clandestine in response to white scrutiny.

❧ 27 ❧

AN ASPECT OF SUCH A PROCESS OF CLANDESTINITY MAY HAVE been the cloaking of thoughts and behaviors in surfacely "pathological" behavioral presentations. This cloaking was a means for ensuring the clandestinity of valued cultural and ethical practices. Under such a strategy, white observers would see only sickness and deviance instead of self and cultural preservation.

Jones (1985) has methodically documented the extent to which white Americans made normal family life problematic for blacks, and the enormous efforts black women made to preserve and create viable family structures and experiences. Assuming an absence of familial bonds from the beginning, all of the attempts made by government to ameliorate the so-called deficiencies in black domestic organization were actually assaults against the method black fathers and moethers were employing to establish some semblance of family life for their children. Black resistance movements during slavery were largely shaped by blacks' overwhelming need to take whatever steps were possible to preclude the break-up of families. From the "get-go" to the present, individual welfare has been conceived communally; communal and family attachment has always been seen as the primary means to individual well-being.

It is possible that blacks exaggerated perceived and existent cultural discrepancies in order to use the exhibition of their interpreted weaknesses as the vehicle to sustain other domestic, kinship, and social practices. In other words, blacks played on the white tendency to see those practices of everyday life which differed from theirs as inadequacies. Knowing that whites would then act to intensify and manipulate those weaknesses in order to increase the efficacy of black subjugation, it is possible that blacks could have wittingly or unwittingly amplified those differences in order to keep white attention away from the fundmental socio-cultural foundations. Even though blacks appeared incapable of constituting nuclear domestic family structures—largely a result of the white organization of slave-quarter society—blacks may have seized upon this point of divergence, exagerrated it, and acted it out in order to preserve the viability, of larger kinship networks and inter-kin relationships.

Instead of protecting and cultivating larger communal ties through the consciously declared valuation of these ties, it is possible that these ties were protected and maintained by individuals continuously attempting and failing at normative nuclear family life. Whites, then, would notice the failure of the black family, and that failure would provide a cover for the continuation of valued forms of domestic organization.

Such a conclusion heuristically makes sense, given the processes through which black kinship systems, in their various interfacings and penetrations of white society, unconsciously and strategically expose each family member to a series of different positions in relationship to white society. A common black strategy has been to use one member's "exposure" to white society as a means of concealing the aspirations, attainments, and behaviors of others. Various family members at different times are isolated, enjoined, covered for, set up, sacrificed, and removed in the kin's dealings with the white world. What has repeatedly impressed me in my sixteen years of clinical psychological practice with black extended-family networks is the degree of variation and versatility employed in the types of exposures and interfaces family members have with whites. Positions of confinement, withdrawal, advancement, high visibility, marginalization, and assimilation are traded off among kinship members—a circulation which seems to avail the larger kinship system (if not individual members or subgroups) to multiple channels of information concerning the overall status of the kin group with white society. For the black family network, the assessment of race relations is to be conducted through the cross-referencings of various informations generated by the multiplicity of types of contact kin members have with whites in a variety of settings. For example, the knowledge gained by a daughter teaching in a university is cross-checked by a mother who is admitted to a hospital for psychiatric evaluation, which is in turn cross-referenced by a cousin who is released from incarceration, which is cross-referenced by another cousin who has been living in a white area now moving back for a short while into the home of the mother and daughter, etc. Each position, as a conceivable place from where blacks can find themselves operating, is used to provide an aspect of the evaluation of every other place in terms of shaping the expectations, cognitions, behaviors, and feelings that are reasonable in any and all places. In the maintenance of communal reference and attachment, each individual's behavioral performance and experience is to be registered and conceived in terms of the experiences of the significant others. Stack (1974) has provided many important insights into how this communalism functions on a material and care-provision level. Much work is yet needed on the construal of the cognitive interweavings I have outlined here.

In contrast to white household organization, consanguinity predominates over conjugality in much of the Black World. The conjugal marriage tends to be highly dependent on external factors and a thorough economic interdependency with extended family networks. Primary relationships have been historically externalized into a larger community life, to ensure that caretaking functions are distributed widely. Sometimes this externalization results in compensatory actions such as the "inventing" of kin, where close non-blood related affiliates are designated as cousin, uncles, and aunts (Aschenbrenner, 1974). Contrary to a former, widely held belief that the volatility of black conjugal relationships represented either intrinsic deficiencies in black kinship and domestic structures or only the severity of assaults leveled against black family structures, the vulnerability of marriage may have, itself, acted to solidify extended family ties when such ties experienced periods of vulnerability. The vulnerability of extended family ties has increased as American society has progressively moved away from acknowledging or sanctioning the importance of extended family functioning, instead shaping forms of economic production which demand individual residential and career mobility. The material independence of the individual household and the dual-career household are also factors which mitigate the sustenance of extended-family ties.

The exclusion from or underemployment of blacks in the work place, the limited access of blacks to quality education and training resources, the migratory patterns of black workers, and the paternalism of the welfare state have contributed to the vast difficulties blacks have had in organizing viable family experiences. However, observers must be careful not to conclude the incapacitation of blacks' ability or desire to provide maternal and psychological care, raise children, produce and circulate information, share resources, love, or create a universe of mutual belonging.

White Americans have tended to believe that if a child is not receiving the care of the natural father and mother at least a few hours everyday, she is not receiving real care or fundamental training (Boykins, et al., 1979; English, 1974; Engram, 1982; McAdoo,1981; Stack, 1974; Sudarkasa ,1981). Many have demonstrated the fallability of such conclusions and have demonstrated that most blacks have had access to some experience of intactness in domestic organizations, even if it did not include the biological parents as primary participants. Some of the supposed deficits in black care-taking and domestic arrangements may actually be seen as strengths, e.g., access to multiple adult caretakers and influences, circumvention of unmalleable caretaker-child alliances which often impede self-development in the "nuclearized" family.

What I am suggesting is that blacks may have taken advantage of the various misperceptions concerning their domestic capabilities by amplifying the separation of married life from the larger kinship networks which it was co-incidental to. By fronting adherence to the standard American norm, blacks continued to fulfill individual responsibilities to kin, but in such a way that it would appear that the surfacely disembodied marriage was indeed the actual and primary experience of black domestic life. In this manner, a form of resistance to the very real and substantial assaults against black family life may have been achieved.

❧ 28 ❧

IT IS IMPORTANT TO KEEP IN MIND THAT WHITE POWER ONCE operated through the constant threat of loss slaveholders held up to their black charges. Slave quarters constantly debated how best to deal with whites. Strategies that permitted continuity and consistency in child-raising inevitably were the one agreed to, resulting in frequent acquiescence to white demands. All throughout slavery, blacks possessed a pervasive antipathy toward whites, despite the power and privileges of the masters. The emphasis on communality and extended family ties is derivable partly by the ability of blacks to deny whites access to the inner workings of slave-quarter life (Genovese, 1972; Webber, 1978; Whitten and Szwed, 1970).

Blacks saw through white moral, religious, and secular teachings. The white attempt to inculcate the superiority and efficacy of its values and world views had the opposite effect: it revealed the fundamental weaknesses in the white position. Despite the fact that the preservation of black religiosity necessitated the adoption of Christian practice, the emphasis on mercy, comfort, liberation, and justice was totally removed from white preoccupations with hell, damnation, and the apocalypse (Webber, 1978). The difference in emphasis ensured that blacks would not be deterred from seeking liberation. No matter what tricks, assaults, and manipulations were applied in attempts to alter their thinking and cultural conceptions, their ways of understanding the world and what was required for their extrication from social and psychological bondage would be steadfastly adhered to.

The white preoccupation with apocalypse led whites to see danger everywhere. A cycle of punishment was instituted largely based on this sense of omnipotent danger and the resultant need to defend against it. White unwillingness to respect and learn from cultural differences made slaves unwilling to allow whites to view what was going on within slave quarters. This, in turn, precipitated an increase of fear and resentment in the white sectors.

If attempts were made to retain an entire array of cultural practices and values from Africa, slave quarters would have been subjected to constant assaults. until the memory and willingness to adhere to such practices were totally eradicated. Instead, blacks always acted as if a substantial portion of their past cultural life was being relinquished in favor of the wisdom and reasonableness of white ways. Repeated simulations, however, have a way of becoming real. The exigency of appearing normal to white scrutiny precluded the frequent use of indigenous languages, religions, and rituals, and did result in a substantial reduction of cultural memory. Yet, the alternation of attenuation with persistence, the giving up of forms and practices that could be converted, reinvoked, and reapplied through white articulations and symbolic structures detracted even the most vigilant white observers from penetrating into the "'interior'" of slave culture. This detraction enabled the maintenance and renewal of certain africentric cultural products. In the long run, what became important to remember was not that much to remember. What was important were ideas, values, and conceptions that could be relayed in touches and glances, messages of togetherness, a sense of "seeing" with the world which is passed on generation to generation. There are words to be whispered, hair to be burned, sayings to be repeated and played with. "When does the African study," asks Blyden (1967: 173). "He studies every day, morning, noon, and night—from the cradle to the grave— he is ever reading the book of nature; and there is never a page in this book which he is either ashamed or afraid to look at."

This renewal of africanity was a key factor in affecting a radical reduction in white efforts to "train" slaves during the latter part of slavery. Whites decided to reduce such efforts because blacks had great success resisting them. A solidified black ethos threatened to challenge white beliefs about the absence of a black culture and thus undermine the ideological rationale used to justify the need for slavery, i.e., as providing a way of life for a people who had no way of life.

The presence of literate and well-traveled Muslims, such as Abdul Rahaman, Mohammed Kaba, Salih Bilali, Job Ben Solomon, and Omar ibn Said suggests the presence of resources within the black quarters who possessed a knowledge of books, a knowledge of West African history, and a capacity to write and, therefore, transmit knowledge to other quarters.

These Muslims were also familiar with Christian myths and principles (Austin 1984). Such resources could have greatly aided the forms and strategies of revision, perseverance, mnemonic versatility, and accommodation which were accomplished during the first years of slavery.

At the time of emancipation, freedom from enslavement was perhaps the most effective assault leveled at blacks' capacity to hold together a vibrant, coherent, and homogeneous black culture. According to Levine (1977), freedom produced a heightened and heretofore-absent self-consciousness about black cultural traditions, which were perceived by many blacks as potentially impeding their ability to take full advantage of the new worlds open to them. It is important to keep in mind that their own prior exclusion from American society was attributed to cultural insufficiencies, so there was great pressure on blacks to demonstrate their competence and ability to fulfill all that was required for full participation. As their speech, religious practices, and looks had been an object of mockery and derision, many backs were quick to attenuate those aspects of themselves that had served to connote major differences in outlook, world view, education, and cooperativeness.

Although blacks tended to become defensive about many aspects of their expressive culture after emancipation and into the twentieth century, such defensiveness seemed more a calculated position designed so as not to waste opportunities for social advancement or, more importantly, limit access to information and experiences in the wider world than a fully internalized evaluation of that culture. Blacks continued to greatly value their capacity for innovation, the expression and absorption of deep feeling, worship and religiosity, communication, and interpersonal astuteness on the microsocial level (Levine 1977).

The strength of any culture is reflected in its ability to extend itself, open itself to that which is beyond its familiar purview, assimilate new influences, and experience itself in new ways. Given the fact that a new world availed itself to black penetration, it is no indication of cultural weakness that blacks moved to take full advantage of these openings. Regardless of whether Kilson (1976) is correct in her contention that blacks acculturated rapidly to American ideals, values, and structures of social differentiation, the forms and the capacities for this acculturation seem to reflect the sustenance of African orientations. For example, no matter how blacks have looked upon black dialects, put them aside, compartmentalized or denied them, they have survived, grown, become more differentiated from standard speech, and been viewed as a necessary linguistic competence by those assured of their competence in standard English. As black dialects are discovered to have significant phonological and morphological continuities with the Niger-Congo family of languages, their importance among the educated black classes is growing. Additionally, the willingness of many blacks to speak within a standard corpus following emancipation may not have reflected the demise of indigenous cultural formations as previously suspected.

Rather, that attempt to master standard English may have been an outgrowth of a preparedness for bilingualism that had developed in Africa even before slavery.

In terms of the contents, the homogeneity of slave culture may have dissipated. Culture, however, is not located in or subsumable to the contents alone. Price (1978), in an introduction to a series of papers about maroon societies in the Americas, points out that, even when blacks didn't have to deal with white constraints or a white presence, the maroon communities seldom reappropriated African cultural, juridical, or political systems directly. This proves to be the case even when the community was constituted by individuals of the same ethnicity. It was rare that such communities were composed of people of similar ethnic backgrounds. A mixture of groups was favored, reflecting the precarious economies of these communities and their need for the collaboration of Indians, renegade whites, and blacks from other regions capable of speaking the languages of the white enemies of the former white masters.

Levine (1977), in his analysis of the transitions in the contents, styles, and forms of black sacred music, identifies perhaps the most salient aspect so far about the process of black acculturation. This acculturation is more than a matter of wholesale or gradual shifts of loyalties and identifications. The process is more complicated. The assimilation itself, according to Levine, becomes simultaneously an acceptable and viable juncture in which to safely rediscover or rearticulate neglected cultural contents or expressive forms. Assimilated Western constructs posit opportunities to apply or invent africanized styles—the end product always being something new, neither a direct copy of white form or a mimicry of African or slave-quarter fashions. As Levine puts it, "few traits emerge through the vehicle of looking within and without" (189).

Arguments are common about how the impact of colonialism and the economic efforts of post-colonial states to integrate into the world-capitalist system have effectively destroyed the cultural formations and ethos of traditional Africa. Large-scale attempts to resume "authentic" African practices have at times been covers for the despotism and terror of regimes such as that of Mobutu in Zaire and Bongo in Gabon. There is no dispute that the colonial legacy made a seemingly irrevocable mess out of things.

The colonial introduction of cash-crop economies , with (1) the subsequent disruption of nomadic grazing patterns; (2) the deprivation of soil nutrients; (3) the increase in soil acidity; and (4) the dependency on inorganic fertilizer, effectively ruined Sahel agriculture by making it unnecessarily vulnerable to prolonged droughts and desertification. The colonial period left a small middle class to run the state machinery, yet provided them with no extensive skills for enlarging the productive sectors of their economies. Increasingly, the state machinery was relied upon as the primary employer, resulting in the rapid consumption of surplus and increased indebtedness to the Western world. In the absence of a viable agricultural infrastructure, there is a massive convergence of rural people upon the cities. Urban life, already overtaxed, spawns intricate and ramifying interdependencies among the populace which make administrative decision-making and social planning almost impossible. Yet, these indigenous compensatory forms are necessary for the sheer day-to-day survival of the majority of the people. On the surface, there are very few places in Africa where an observer can get an impression of anything working. However, in Africa, there are multiple surfaces, many different, contradictory impressions that should curtail any rush to conclude cultural as well as economic ruin.

Western cultural practices, religions, languages, administrative forms, values, logical structures, and modalities of exchange have been imposed upon Africa. The imposition, however, is itself mediated and interpreted by the people imposed upon. These mediations and interpretations are continuously revised, and the revisions themselves affect alterations in how a people understands itself, what is happening to them, and what outcomes they produce through their actions. Throughout Africa, contact with the West and Western thought did not necessarily make the condition of indigenous peoples more abstract and conceptual but, rather, diminished indigenous forms of abstraction, in turn, prompting greater concreteness. Far from being a closed system free of antagonism and revision, rife with concreteness and literality, and devoid of a capacity for logical and propositional reasoning, traditional forms of African cognition were highly diversified in their complexity (Bauer and Hinnant, 1980; Cole and Scribner, 1974; Fernandez, 1972, 1980).

As Fernandez (1972) states, civilizing missions have not been unilateral in their effects. At times, they invert traditional modes of thought, but with the result that the inversion can reinvigorate the traditional cognitive styles. The imposition of Western orientations may have generated the reassertion of formerly valued understandings of the world and the attempt to locate forms within the dominant culture that vindicated and supported indigenous world-views.

Thus, the rigid distinctions between abstract and concrete thought, often invoked to dismiss the applicability of traditional thought structures to modern situations, are often false, or at least ambiguous. Even in Western science, these distinctions have limited applicability, especially in the fields of physics, telecommunications, and quantum mechanics. When positing a new scientific theory, the Euro-American researcher seldom "unverifies" what passes for true. Rather, when limits of old paradigms are confronted, the solution is often no more than deeming what was impossible in the old paradigm as possible in the new one. Both old and new conceptions become equally true and the two incompatible worlds they suggest are both equally real Moscovici (1981). "Progress" is obtained by the tendency for the new conception to appear as the negation of the old conception. However, the new paradigm incorporates the old as a re-affirmation of the new made in a different universe or arena of discourse.

The applicability of different cognitive structures cannot be evaluated solely in terms of their rational efficacy alone, especially when people have a difficult time finding rationality in their living situations. While living in Mauritania, I often talked to men whose ideas for the resuscitation of the bankrupt economy made absolutely no sense. They claimed, probably quite correctly, that their situation was now beyond rationality. A familiar refrain was: "If there is nothing one can reasonably do about our situation, does this mean we should stop thinking?"

In his study of the resurgence of proverbial forms among the Fang in postcolonial Gabon, Fernandez (1972) notes, "[the iconic] is not simply an abstracting or categorizing linguistic response to a situational dilemma of experience, rather it summons up imagery to deal with a dilemma of experience, and hence is itself exciting to the consciousness whose dilemmas it appears to resolve" (417). During the colonial and post-colonial periods, there was a general tendency toward a complementary distribution of incompatible values, where traditional and contemporary cognitions are assigned and used in different situations as methods of explication and evaluation (Fernandez, 1978; MacGaffey, 1981; Mudimbe, 1983).

What has been striking to me in my discussions with both educated and uneducated Africans is their resiliency in crossing symbolic and literal thresholds, as evidenced in their approach to the concept of self, which they see as an assemblage of dimensions cohered as a vehicle for the articulation and exhibition of an array of life forces. There has been much debate over whether such conceptions are experienced literally or metaphorically. But this is a dilemma that is posited by Euro-American constraints themselves. Many Africans can display a penchant for literality when transitions in the symbolic order prove overly ambiguous, excessive, or confining. They demonstrate an ability to regard and experience these conceptions metaphorically when confronted with discursive and administrative structures which make the traditional distinctions between discrete areas of life and between the important impacting forces (e.g., bush/household, ancestors/sorcerers, city/country) difficult to sustain. This is presently the situation as the need to structure everyday life in terms proximate to Western life has disrupted the ability of Africans to attend fully to the psychological labor needed to keep alive and meaningful the interactions between material and spiritual, familial and public, urban and rural forces. In the African experience, such categorical oppositions are unbalanced; they must be constantly re-established and re-negotiated. Nothing is taken for granted, as all the salient categories, types, and forces intermingle. As a result, the self is exhibited through many different cognitive and linguistic dimensions. Cohered and differentiated through a variation of intensities, as opposed to clearly defined components, the experiences of selfhood disrupt, stretch, and distort the terms and psychologies applied to codify them. If this process is not understood with the literality of precolonial life, much of the parodied and exaggerated displays of both Western habits and traditional custom act to create a metaphorical space for this multiplicity to continue. The often anarchic and repressive ways African states often push to exceed themselves, the hastily negotiated deals with transnationals that deplete or go nowhere, the manipulative improvisations compensating for bureaucratic ineptness, the rampant disregard for borders or legal transactions, and the apparently wasteful expenditures on pomp and frivolous testimony, all contain within them a desire to upend and enlarge every conceivable social, political, interpersonal, and economic relationship.

The self is to be used as an instrument applied to others as a means of freeing the "frozen forces" and static definitions. That is, it is to be used to enable other people to imagine and experience themselves in unprecedented ways. It is what Derrida might call an "asymptotic place of convergences among all possible translations" (1981a).

The Eurocentric emphasis on the precision of interpretation and on the reduction of ambiguity neglects the value and significance of the elusiveness which motivated the move toward the proficiency of interpretive apparatuses to begin with—the thrills of both conceptual release and capture. There is little sense in the African context that one must labor at speech or meaning (Sandywell, et al., 1975). One works only to bring a temporary cessation to the passage of time. Such a cessation is desired precisely because the flow of temporal experience possesses more than enough significance. Therefore, the African seldom feels that she has to cut her losses, or recoup her generativity in the either/or distinctions between metaphorical and rational thought.

As Africa seemingly drifts into an irrevocable paralysis and a harrowing silence, neither the apparent paralysis or silence should be viewed exclusively as the diminution of intellectual resiliency—a resiliency which may be prepared to stand out in an emptiness where there is nothing left but itself.

An example of such versatility is implicitly demonstrated in the fact that the required reading for much of the continent is not Marx, Nkrumah, Diop, or Cabral, but Evelyn Waugh's *Black Mischief,* a banal and weakly sardonic tale written in 1932 about the post-colonial dilemmas of a classic "banana republic." In the book, European delegations are oblivious to all but the disturbances in their baths and don't even notice when they've accidentally eaten one of their own kind. A young black emperor—whose attempts at modernization ("Through sterility to culture" is a standard motto) unleashes the forces of an archaic primitivism—fails to provide the slightest measure of autonomy for his kingdom. The fact that pulp has been elevated to the status of a required text reflects a growing tendency by young, literate Africans to understand the West through its most caricatured representations of African people. Since these Western "understandings" reveal the West as inept, provincial, inflexible, and oblivious, the popularity of the book indicates that the readers are prepared to acknowledge their own "stupidity" as a means of deconstructing the infallibility of Euro-American rationality.

In a series of important researches conducted in various parts of the Third World, Shweder (1984) demonstrates the continued use of sociocentric models by individuals to explain their relationship to a larger social order. The human body is used as a primary metaphor for the thorough integration of the individual into social life—a model of differentiated parts arranged in a hierarchy of functions and servicing the whole. Despite the preference and everyday use of such sociocentric conceptions by Shweder's subjects, they do display, in experimental situations, the capacity for abstraction, assigning conceptual themes and trait descriptions to an array of intrapsychic and social events. Third World peoples still primarily oriented to traditional cultural frameworks thus do what they supposedly couldn't do: abstract generalities from specific daily events. The question becomes why such divergences in modalities of cognition persist if "traditional" peoples are capable of utilizing communicational and cognitive forms that would provide the structural basis for an intersubjective relationship between North and South. The absence of a convergence cannot simply be a matter of a developmental lag.

Furthermore, increased tendencies in conscious elaboration and articulation do not necessarily indicate increases in the complexity of cognition (Caton, 1966, 1981; Cole and Scribner, 1974; Eco, 1976, 1984; Glenn, 1974; Gumperz, 1971, 1982; Hymes, 1974; Scribner and Cole, 1981). The mechanisms of actual conversation do not simply reflect the knowledge and ideas of speakers. Rather, these mechanisms are strategies for the particular use of knowledge, given the social realities speakers perceive they are up against. They are as much a way of concealing cognitive capabilities as they are mechanisms for revealing them. As Tyler (1984) points out, the significance or intelligence of what is said depends on the background of shared or proposed assumptions about the significance of articulated understandings. Yet, these assumptions are only arrived at through an ongoing negotiation of reality in actual conversation and talk.

As Foucault reminds us in *The Order of Things,* "the only thing we know at the moment, in all certainty, is that in Western culture the being of man and the being of language have never, at any time, been able to coexist and to articulate themselves upon the other" (1970: 339).

Both Africans and black Americans refer more to context-specific knowledge or to past conversations than to the ideal generalities or principles evoked through these conversations. Blacks actively refer to what they and others have actually said, recreate the exchange of voices. In this practice knowledge is viewed as the organized trace of a discontinuous series of conversations. It is a summary or convergence of the positions the speaker has assumed with others during a given period of time, an assessment of the courses of action that have become available or foreclosed for both the speaker and others. The focus on forms of talk takes precedence over the ideas expressed. As Goffman (1981) indicates, these forms provide speakers with elbow room to produce and construct ideas and evaluations about what they think is occurring in any interaction. They enable speakers to make their position felt, and make their alignment to what is occurring known without committing or provoking others to address themselves openly to these communications. In this way, talk goes on. Sometimes, in the interest of maintaining or abrupting communication, it is best to say a lot. At other times, it is best to say little, be allusive, aphoristic, or mundanely ritualistic. At no time, however, do these forms indicate what the conversant is capable of thinking. Talk itself, and its concomitant effect upon individuals located and operating in specific social contexts, becomes the means not only of representing these individuals and contexts, but of acting upon and altering the principles of knowledge which organize them.

Wirendu (1976) and Houtondji (1983) worry that the apparent absence of conceptual analysis and metareflexivity, and the elevation of traditional belief systems and cosmologies to the status of an indigenous African philosophy, will leave Africans without a rigorous proficiency in the application of formal thought systems. For them, the only real philosophy is the philosophy of Marx, Hegel, and Althusser. Written textuality is viewed as the sole purveyor of philosophical thought, and they worry about the historical deficiencies that have ensued from the absence of writing systems on the continent. (They neglect to consider the extensive hieroglyphic systems that did exist in Africa, even though these systems were primarily invocational rather than representational).

Although it is possible to appreciate the concern of these two African philosophers (a concern shared by many African intellectuals), the emphasis on the generation of a systematized body of philosophical texts may be more a practical, rather than philosophical, exigency. The concern, perhaps, overestimates the rigor, sacrosanctity, and totalizing impact of Euro-American systems of rationality—systems whose authority is increasingly challenged by Western thought itself (Bloor, 1970; Scholte, 1981). Both Wirendu and Houtondji neglect to focus on the circumstances that allow for the prioritization of rational thought and fail to consider that whether to write or not to write may be a choice emanating from a philosophical position rather than simply a reflection of cultural incompetence.

As I emphasize to black students whose writing skills reflect an apparent plethora of deficiencies, the importance of writing "well" (according to traditional academic standards) is to be able to legitimately, without anxiety or self-doubt, write "bad" again. That is, the apparent deficiencies represent both the lack of comprehensive training and a resistance to being fully incorporated into the standards through which expressive performance is normalized.

To put feelings and thoughts in the forms one is taught is, in some way, to give them up to a system of authorities mostly mistrusted. Now you have it, i.e., the expression of your viewpoint and life situation, and then, once it is commanded into acceptable modalities of presentation and reflection, you don't. Kids in classrooms are often asked to say what's on their mind, especially when they demonstrate some form of unwillingness to go along with the program. When they say it in a way that perhaps represents the self-perceived singularity of their life situation, they are often instructed to re-present it in a way that closes out many of the realities the kid is up against. The outside is not allowed to make sense in school, and so school stops making sense to the kid. This process in no way accounts for the whole picture concerning the difficulties many black kids have in acquiring basic skills, but it is an important piece. Caught in the interstices between an unacknowledged supplement of expressive capacities and the acknowledged absence of viable expressive performance, many black students end up doubting the entirety of their linguistic and expressive competencies.

Similarly, as long as Africa is caught in a twilight zone of doubt about its own cultural formations and its efficacious use of Western constructs, it will be unable to cultivate the generative capacities needed to develop either indigenous or assimilated constructs. The predominance of

Western techno-rationality renders any attempt to cultivate, extend, and elaborate traditional knowledges an apparent move backward, despite the fact that traditional society has never been a closed system and the fact that the theoretical implosions of the postmodern era make the traditional look modern and the modern look traditional.

Additionally, the *imposition,* rather than the *proposition,* of development through technology has generated a continuous resistance to the full incorporation and use of technological instruments—a resistance often distorted by the lack of an adequate material base for the incorporation of these instruments. It is important to restore the instrumentality of indigenous formations. This is not to be done through an articulation of a hopefully intact cultural memory and resurrection of artifacts and propositions—the soul of culture does not rest here anyway. Rather, this restoration is best done by elaborating ways in which Western culture could be appropriated as a reinforcement of valued cultural processes, and by looking at how such processes can be enunciated through technological development. The question becomes whether the uses of technological developments are necessarily limited to the logic of action and speed utilized by Western operators, and whether there exist African tactics of utilization that might begin to counter the political and economic marginalization of Africa.

❀ 31 ❀

THERE IS A TENDENCY IN SOME QUARTERS OF THE BLACK World to believe that a reversion to an intact tradition is the cure for a failed modernity. Regarded in this way, such re-invocations may act as repressive forces, often scapegoating the very enunciations and activities that have the best chance of forming a bridge between a toolbox of traditional cultural instruments and the fuzzy, yet distinct, shapings of a reawakened cultural imagination. Such repressive tendencies can be seen in the attack upon women's autonomy and productive capabilities in several African nations under the guise of a return to traditional values. Unmarried women over thirty are being banned from many Nigerian cities, forced into prostitution to support families, and then chastised for their immorality.

Since women have historically managed agricultural production and, in many cases, are the only farmers now that men have gravitated toward the towns and cities, the assault upon.:the limited independence they have achieved during the post-colonial period can be viewed as an attempt to undermine their productive capacities so that the parastatal and/or private sector can institute export-oriented agriculture on corporate farms. With many young women simultaneously rooted in traditional modes of economic production and in nascent forms of gender networking that are producing new forms of social consciousness and exchange, it is women who are, theoretically, in the best position to reconceptualize African society. Yet, it is women who are under attack. A sense of cultural nationalism is crucial for them but, at the same time, it cannot be accomplished through the denial of their free agency.

Cultural tradition is not a coherent, intact body of thoughts and world views that can be appropriated into any place with full comprehension. The inability to make sense of traditions often becomes *the* sense of an individual's relationship with them. This irony propels young African women to insist upon resiliency in how their traditions are interpreted. The absence of precise understanding does not undermine a contemporary relationship with tradition; it simply means that present usages of tradition are not bound to any over-arching guidelines, specifications of success or failure. The erasure of past cultural meanings does not erase the possibilities of finding meaning in attempts to respond to values produced by ancestors.

There has been much lost in Africa. As in the case of a lost loved one, the loss is neither to be accepted, rejected, or simply compensated for. The loss of traditional value reveals the madness of that which the tradition promised, i.e., the circumvention of loss—what tradition must promise but which no tradition can deliver. Tradition's loss propels those who valued it into resigning themselves to the impossibility of a coherent universe.

Nevertheless, meaning is more than merely the erasure of meaning (Derrida, 1981). The accordance of authoritative and specific meanings to cultural traditions is the very undoing of these traditions. Myths:of omnipotence and perfection kill tradition. Instead, the willingness to forget the specific values, uses, orders, and significations of these traditions becomes a sign of their ongoing forcefulness. Apostel (1981) points out that cultures which attempt to preserve cultural memory at all costs are usually the first ones to lose it. Culture is most powerful when it is heuristic rather than prescriptive. Derrida, in all of his work, has emphasized that it is more functional to approach cultural formations in terms of what they might or could be saying. Then, the individual and/or culture must act with and through a broad range of meanings. Only in this spirit of speculation can the forcefulness, suggestivity, and usefulness of a cultural tradition be more than an institutionalized and interminable mourning for past life.

Oppression is not simply the erosion or homogenization of cultural differences. It includes confining the consideration of distinct cultural formations to a reading of their surfaces, of what can be counted, grouped, classified, timed, recorded, photographed, or measured. Everything that is important to know is too often seen as readily or potentially apparent. Further penetration is not considered because the entirety of what is of value is viewed to be fully present on the surface of bodies, signs, and actions. Caricatured, fractured, and displaced images of sociality derived from such reading can only be thought of as a well-ordered system of hierarchical levels or else a hodgepodge of irreconcilable stances, slogans, cures, evils, pasts, and futures. Everything is to be compared and contrasted as manifestations of universal principles which are, themselves, compared and contrasted. What ensues from this framework is the conviction that all behaviors, communications, and cultural productions are subsumable within an over-arching rubric of human development—there is only one course of modernity, progress, one standard of optimum performance, intelligence, and value.

At the same time, this reading of cultural surfaces makes people suspicious and resistant to accepting what is presented at face value, and instead ushers in a reading which dives off the deep end, plumbs subterranean layers of meaning for the definitive connections and complicities, and wallows in an endless indeterminacy of meaning. There is too much to figure out; any idea, behavior, or event could mean too many things. Innovative action is made impossible and is condemned with the sense that there are no viable suggestions or possibilities worth paying attention to. Here, there are no pasts or futures, no development or progress. The delving into the deep simply enhances the desirability and legitimacy of surface readings, provides these readings with an economy of high cost-effectiveness. One reads the cultural surfaces as "either this specific thing or nothing at all." The surface becomes the only thing that can be trusted and read without undermining the practice of reading itself, i.e., the assuredness of interpretation and comprehension. Texts may possess a fundamental heterogeneity of voices and articulate multiple speech communities, but the *designation* of heterogeneity and the *mark* of multiplicity, on the level of reading culture, tend to supercede the experiencing of heterogeneous voices themselves.

In the postmodern context, we read among depths only at our own risk—the risk of knowing nothing. This is an era where every surface becomes a surface of information, where the economy produces surfaces capable of storing and transferring information to other surfaces, and where the distances between discrete surfaces become irrelevant in terms of this transfer. Acting on the terror of knowing nothing, we conclude, without difficulty, that we know nothing. The more we know, the more we feel we lack the important knowledge and need to know more. The more we pursue this additional knowledge, the more highlighted become the inadequacies of any knowledge. Soon we conclude the inevitability of (and perhaps preference for) our own stupidity. This conclusion typically mitigates our connections with the world and any possible challenges to the old conventions. Despite the slogan of a recent advertisement for the newspaper, *U.S. Star*—"the more you read, the more you are involved,"—the more we as a culture read, the less we want to be involved.

As a Diallobe king tells a Western school master in Chiek Hamidou Kane's book, *Ambiguous Adventure,* "Your science is the triumph of evidence, a proliferation of the surface. It makes you the masters of the external, but at the same time it exiles you there more and more" (78).

In traditional African cultures, the surfaces, depths, and beyonds were barely distinguishable from each other. Oscillating the demarcations with his own movements, man was simultaneously located in every dimension. Imprecision, fuzziness, and incomprehension were the very conditions which made it possible to develop a viable knowledge of social relations. Instead of these conditions being a problem to be solved by a resolute knowledge, they were viewed as the necessary limits to knowledge itself, determined the value with which such knowledge was held, and the attitudes taken toward it.

There were choices among readings to be made. People looked for the best way to read things. That chosen as the best was not viewed as inherently the best to the exclusion of other readings. The best was one that added resiliency, validation, or sustenance to the *act* of reading. Africans did consider every surface as a surface to be read. Each reading was to add something else that could be said, neither to the detriment, exclusion, or undoing of any other reading. Not all surfaces were visible.

The position of being an individual with a capacity to articulate freely is expressed by the Songhai of Mali as : "I am a voice from elsewhere free to say exactly what they want." Here, the content of what is said is free of the particular act of speaking, and vice-versa. As such, no one can determine who the speaker really is, yet everyone knows that a speaker does exist, is speaking, and that a particular kind of speaker is, at least, speaking the reality of a particular speaker even if the speaker who speaks can never be reduced to the reality spoken. "They (the gods, ancestors, others) want it said, not me, and when they want to speak, this want has nothing to do with what I, as a speaker in my own right, might want." Because he voices the thoughts of others, the speaker is not implicated, constrained, or held back in the speaking. His freedom to speak is not contingent upon what he has to say. He can make something happen—invent, undermine, posit, play—without it seeming that he is the one doing it. The speaker is not to be located in the situation he represents or creates with his speech and its concomitant assumptions and ideas. Some part of the speaker is always some place else. Therefore, no matter what happens as a result of the speaking, he is never fully captured, analyzed, apprehended, or pinned down by the listeners. Although this notion sounds like a Western deconstructive position toward identity in general, the difference in the Songhai context is that this notion is consciously recognized as the precondition for speaking in general and descriptive of the psychological orientation assumed toward speaking.

The viability of traditional cultural formations could be viewed in a way similar to the above Songhai psychology. Such traditions speak with authority and guidance only through the attempts of individual members of culture to maximize the resiliency of their dealings with the multiple dimensions of a social body. Such resiliency is obtained only through the mutual respect accorded by both the culture and individual to alternative possibilities in how the relationship between them can be conceptualized and read. Neither will be fully explicable to the other. However, the willingness of both to produce for the other is based on this very inexplicability, on the fact that particular readings don't belong to either cultures or individuals.

The current sense of disconnection from and doubt about cultural traditions in Africa is experienced as particularly troubling in large part because of the nature of these traditions. In many African cultures, progress was traditionally viewed as something the culture had already obtained in the past, the future being seen as the possibility of recognizing the moral achievements of the past—achievements that were not cognizant to those ancestors, now dead, who had achieved them. The living were assured of the immanence of such a recognition because the ancestors (lives now enriched by death) were always "available" to guide the living toward that recognition—the communication between worlds being direct and incessant (Zahan 1979). With this confidence, the culture could take many risks in its thinking, expressions and assumptions about itself, abandon one set of principles for the invention of others. These intentions enabled the living to continuously challenge and motivate the ancestors and gods to say something about themselves and to negotiate new arrangements for speaking with each other.

By turning the noncontingent connection between past and present into one that had to make itself known through representation, the African confidence in risk and abandonment was severely depleted. An openness to the unknown had to be converted into the expulsion of a foreign body that constricted the sense of psychological and spiritual mobility which had formerly imbued the African self with its instrumentality. Africans were put in the position where the survival of their cultures necessitated actions which countered the vitality of these cultures, i.e., Africans could no longer afford to be open to the outside when that outside (European colonialism) threatened to wipe out traditional cultures altogether. Under the gaze and imposition of a Eurocentric administrative apparatus, the economic and social activities that sprang from the irreducible oscillation of the visible and invisible, the sensible and the ridiculous, the light and shadows, the friend and enemy, and the village and bush were destroyed.

It is important to consider the vast array of frameworks through which the imposition of colonialism was interpreted and responded to, the ways in which the colonial gaze was deflected and returned—how Europeans themselves were watched. What Africa lacks is not so much a counter-knowledge to Western constructs but a viable apparatus for compiling and distributing this knowledge, for making it known. In the rush to either join or extricate itself from the West, Africa does not pay sufficient attention to how indigenous bodies of thought evaluate the consequences of massive cultural disruptions. Few people pay attention to what Africans themselves did and are doing to create spaces of cultural autonomy. With its back against the wall, it is important for Africa to take risks because only in risk-taking can a sense of self-confidence and self-reliance be restored, and its dependency on outside interests lessened. Nyerere's refusal to accede to IMF demands, the construction of a new system of agricultural production in Burkina Faso, and the maintenance of open borders in the Sudan are small signs of such a capacity for risk-taking.

❀ 32 ❀

THE COMMON ASSUMPTION HAS BEEN THAT THE CULTURES OF the Black World have been exploited and dominated out of existence. As Fanon put it, traditional culture becomes uninhabitable. Certainly much has been lost. But as has been mentioned previously, much of the loss is only apparent, as the mode of preservation, refinement, and rearticulation have often necessitated:

1. blacks acting as if assimilation was both desired and total;

2. psychological maroonage, where blacks cloaked valued processes through the occupation of social and psychological characteristics considered pathological by whites

and;

3. a willingness to reconcile Eurocentric and Africentric orientations, as evidenced by the full incorporation of mulattos into African American culture during the early decades of the twentieth century.

Fanon's injunction for critical observers to look for racism at all levels of sociality may obscure discernment of the ways the Black World has been circumventing, mediating, and counter-manipulating that racism for several centuries. During American slavery, the position of social inferiority was not necessarily translated by blacks into feelings of moral or psychological inferiority. The limited efficacy of overt resistance did not deter blacks from thinking that, in the long run, it was they, not whites, who possessed the strategic advantage—as indicated in a popular saying at the time, "de buckruh hab scheme, en de nigger has trick, en ebry time de buckruh scheme once, de nigger trick twice" (Webber, 1978). Another slave-quarter saying, "it is a poor dog that won't wag its own tail," reflected a widely-held belief that the white need for the institution of slavery made the white man inferior, motivating slaves to maintain and cultivate separate values and ways of understanding the world.

Even though Fanon (1967) insists that the only option for the oppressed is to "fling himself upon the imposed culture with the desperation of a drowning man" (39), the degree of inferiority depends on the references used, the site in which it is felt and derived. The same oppression which levels and flattens can also be experienced as evidence for an enduring, unyielding strength or indifference.

157

The Black World may not have been able to shake loose the grip of white exploitation, but in substantial ways it has established the terms for how that grip will mean for both black and white hands.

Through the re-workings of outlooks and customs, the formation of indigenous pedagogies, and the strategies for assimilating the outside and deploying the inside, the those in the Black World have engaged in endless struggles over the definition of what their lives and blackness will mean. In a way perhaps similar to the function of urban social movements, the attempts to maintain viable cultural distinctions keep alive the Black World's capacity to imagine an undominated fruition and to live within existing dominations equipped with a determination to do more than survive (Castells 1983).

The tendency of progressive political discourses to posit the Black World as primarily the victim of exploitation fails to assert that much more is occurring. To see exploitation, while neglecting to acknowledge the many ways the Black World continues to replenish and nurture itself becomes simply another means of denying its value, thinking, and feeling. As such, these citations of exploitation exist as another manifestation of a racial apparatus that diminishes the applicability of black cultural productions to white lives.

Since victimage is a position that can, with conceivable justification, be claimed by all people in one way or another, claims of an enhanced morality and a right to reparations, or demands for a distinct evaluative framework for legal, psychological, or policy judgements now act with diminished rhetorical force. Recent adolescent markings on subway advertisements—"victim shoes, victim hair, victim clothes" —reflect several aspects of a response to both the emasculation of victimage and the ways its public presentation and sexualization through forms of dress and "media-celebrated" submissions assert that defilement is the privilege of wealth and status. Young kids of color, by announcing their intention to victimize those perceived as making it in the larger society, attempt to recoup their own status as victims—a status which they will deny as long as it is presented as an essential connotation of high style filled with sadomasochistic motifs.

If they hunt and prowl, rather than subject themselves to the paltry manifestations of a receding interest in their situations, they are no longer the victims, even if, in the larger scheme of their capacities to function and thrive, this particular strategy intensifies their victimage. Kids take to the street as a means of commanding respect. The respect is vanquished, however, by systems of justice, which, unable to respect their own principles and functions, render the issue of respect an increasingly driven and desperate one for those now in the perpetual shuttle between street and prison. Persistent, respect becomes something to be won at all costs.

To know oneself as victim is to know that it is exceedingly difficult to know oneself as anything else. The wounding is predominant and permanent. Even if a life is made out of the hypervisibility of the wounding and the "victim" laughs all the way to the bank, it will always be known as a life that was not really preferred. There are some kids who are so thoroughly constituted as victims that they resist cooperation with any person who talks about their victimage. They demand to be viewed as the hunters and "savages" that the general population, preoccupied with crime and safety, is more than willing to see them as. At times, youth diversion and counseling projects which attempt to keep juveniles outside the justice system and deter hardcore criminal participation have minimal impact because they are perceived by some kids as attempts to deprive them of their status as dangerous—a status they feel committed to as the only way of guaranteeing the accordance of respect.

In the realm of black subjectivity, there are many knowledges for sure, many ways blacks have made their subjection and subjectivity sensible to themselves. There is both exploitation and strategic responses to that exploitation which have enabled the Black World to sustain and invent experiences for itself that differ from the experiences intended for it by white domination. Blacks have always tried to understand and experience their lives as more than exploitation. As black Americans frequently point out, white people just don't know how to *see*. That is, they don't know how to place themselves in the wholeness of a situation, don't know how to view themselves through the lens of a situation in its entirety as opposed to viewing others as if the observer always assumed the central position.

Even in the silence of near-starvation in the Sahel, children invent new games, husbands tell their wives about their dreams, and the women stand in circles giving birth to new spirits. Death and corruption may be certain, but what comes after that is not. What comes after is a place worth addressing and living for, a place that respects the dignity of the emaciated, that accepts the curiosity of those under the guns of invisible wars.

What is needed is a different language in which to speak about oppression. No matter how sufficient presently available discourses may be in explaining the production and structuration of social domination, present references to a divided social body seem frequently foolish in light of the oppressed's "victory" in the politics of conversation, i.e., more and more people, regardless of their social standing, are persuaded that they are oppressed. In fact, there are those who believe that the incarcerated underclass have it better than they do—three square meals a day, plenty of drugs, no work.

One young lawyer told me, "Here I work my butt off to get a good education and a good job, and I hardly have time to do anything I want to do... sometimes I think about taking a walk at three in the morning but I'm scared to think what would happen to me... at least those kids can go anywhere they want at any time of day... they may not amount to much but, look it, they can pretty much do any-thing they want; they don't have to work or go to school, all they gotta put up with is the fact that there's not gonna be much else for them; sometimes I think, hell, if I could put up with it, it wouldn't be that hard doing what they do; hell, if I make one wrong move here in this place (the district attorney's office) my career would be over just like that."

It is necessary to emphasize *both* the existence of

black exploitation and black strength and resiliency. Neither can be discussed in isolation from the other. They are inseparable dimensions of the functioning of a racial apparatus which acts to cancel the contributions of black culture through exploitation. Additionally, the operations of exploitative mechanisms are continuously improved on the basis of an implicit recognition of black strengths by whites. Denial affirms and affirmation denies.

Perhaps the tendency to insist upon the intensity of exploitation in the Black World serves to counter the thinking exemplified by the lawyer above, who sees indications of the good life in desperate experiences. The ease through which such inversions can now take place is an important warning to any attempt to assert that exploitation can be a positive experience for the recipients. The critical observer must always acknowledge the positive capacities which ensue from attempts to attenuate or mediate exploitation, but must also never lose sight of the fundamental disparities in advantage and privilege which exist between white and black worlds. Neither should this observer reduce these disparities to suprasensible positions such as "exploiter-victim," with their "promises" of an immanent upending. The interconnections are no longer ones of good guy versus bad guy; the collusions are more intricate, the influences mutual and reverberating.

5

The End of Racism Means
Knowing How to Die

❁ 33 ❁

IN STREET, CRIMINAL, AND TELEVISION VERNACULARS, "TO
waste" is to kill, to make refuse out of the living. This
metaphor for death and the orientation of Euro-American
attitudes toward death may address basic issues related to
white racism.

Distinctions between First and Third World epistemologies have traditionally been most striking when applied to death. As Minister Louis Farrakhan indicated in his

radio address of November 18, 1984, "the trouble with the white man is that he is so preoccupied with death, that he doesn't know how to die." Not knowing precisely what Farrakhan had in mind, I do think he speaks forcefully to the West's anxiety about the possibilities of its own immobility and stagnation.

In Euro-American analytical systems, knowledge has been obtained by extracting the object of attention from its ongoingness within a fluid environment, where the fluidity itself is controlled in research regimens that decide what is extraneous or insignificant to the identified area of functioning in question. In many respects, to know is to freeze, to stop the mobility of the organism by isolating it, getting it to reflect upon its movements, or counting its responses in a simulated environment. So far, magnification of the organism and its components, dissection, measurement, and attribution have necessitated stillness. Even naturalistic methodologies propose the order of the structures "observed."

To know someone has often meant the refusal to be surprised by their actions. Deviations are often registered as no more than moments of waywardness from a basic essence. To be known, then, is perceived by Western subjects with the relief that they belong somewhere but also with the terror that somehow they are captured, held, and denied an opportunity to be something entirely different. Cohered in the clinical gazes of others, the individual feels drained of the motivation to use and be swayed by other configurations of conceivable existence. She feels the loss of the perpetually unspecifiable and uncodifiable desires that once enabled her to feel and live out the singularity of her being.

To be known is to be subsumed into comparisons, categories, and classifications which tend to deny the person her subjectivity. Power defines, rendering persons worthy or unworthy of the attentions of others; it prescribes territories of operation. Knowledge of self is made to imitate a system of surveillance: we watch ourselves. Our self-consciousness steers us into identifiable and predictable parameters of action—we diminish risk-taking, flexibility, and impetuousness; restrict the universe of possibility.

Our knowledge of ourselves incorporates death as a necessity for a proper understanding of living. Understanding this capacity to be rendered immobile, the Western self rushes madly to vacate social positions which become too familiar — "I must bc something else; I must keep moving." Postmodern culture moves to render obsolete what is currently valued. Newness becomes the primary consumable item. For something to be new and "attractive," or viable as new, the present must be turned into refuse, must be wasted. To make waste (to make dead) becomes the strategy of compensation for Western fears concerning death. To be stuck in a rut doing the same old thing is a major psychological worry of postmodern America. It takes precedence over desires for security or stable relationships.

More precisely, the current preference is for safe risk-taking, stable and incessant self transformations. This preference increasingly acculturates persons to perpetual states of crisis in domestic and affective relationships, institutional functioning, and political and economic life. Crisis becomes the insurance of stability. In therapeutic situations, I have worked with couples who are unable to function without constant exposure to accidents, calamity, and external threats to the sustenance of the relationship. The couples move among a succession of court dates, hospital emergency rooms, unemployment offices, and police stations. Here, movement is a shuffling of bureaucratic designations.

In postmodern America both crisis and stability are wasted. The irruptive value of crisis is wasted by crisis functioning as a homeostatic mechanism. The mutual understanding and solidity of the couple is wasted by their constant vulnerability to disruption—stability and irruption cancel the other out. Similarly, the process whereby the old "regime" is vacated in favor of the new expires the freshness and vitality of the new forms occupied because the individual already anticipates their eventual, and probably rapid, exhaustion. A "living" space is thus wasted, made dead, so that a space of death might be occupied, i.e, the old is killed off so that the new might be made old. These notions don't mean that actual change is neither desirable or possible. Living seems to imply constant fluidity and malleability. Rather, it is the worry and fear about individual immobility which tend to obscure and mitigate attention to the value and nurturance of the forms, styles, and modes of living presently occupied. Instead of applying what is familiar in variegated ways, Western selves rush to kill off such forms and styles, languages and articulations, relationships and belongings, before they expend themselves or last for a lifetime.

What is most self-defeating is that this preoccupation with possible immobility often eventuates in the stuckness feared. By endlessly producing possibilities for consuming the new, the perception of stuckness is amplified even when individuals are indeed going through changes. Exposed to an infinite variety of lifestyles and retreats, individuals cling more tightly to what is presently in operation, perhaps sensing that whatever is changed will have to be changed time and time again, so it is better to stay where one is.

The open-endedness of the future is thus perceived as already over before it is even conceived, or is conceived as a creation already dead, its value and forcefulness already known. Frequently I hear clients account for their reluctance to change jobs, lovers, or places of residence by saying that it is too much work for something they already know the outcome of. With this attitude, differences are reduced to ground zero. Death is actually looked forward to as the beginning of real difference.

Without a sense of freshness or open-endedness accompanying the changes increasingly obligated, the driven need to change, reform, or rehabilitate the self usually means that the change is never affected. When the urgency for change takes precedence over the imagining of what one might be, that which is old, wasted, and dead must be kept alive and near in order for the individual to determine just how much she has changed. But in this reference "backward," where the maintenance of the old self is the confirmation of its own abandonment, the change really never goes anywhere. It is linked, referred, and tied to that which has already received its death sentence. The harder the self tries to change, the more she will find herself unable to do so. Taking this inability out on herself, the individual criticizes and further wounds her capacities, and increases the urgency of the change at the same time as making her less likely to accomplish it.

In the urgency of the West to be itself, the contributions of other cultures are belittled—contributions that originally enabled the West to be what it is. Denying the saliency of those others, Western culture finds itself unable to be satisfied or fulfilled in anything it knows about itself. It views that dissatisfaction as emanating from either its contamination by those others or its lack of will to convert those others into opportunities for its own self-recognition. Thus, the West simultaneously excludes and incorporates. It attempts to exclude death by incorporating death as the basis for self-knowledge; it incorporates death, excluding it as something to be lived and acknowledged in the present.

In turn, Euro-American culture has utilized this orientation to death as the model through which it relates to people of color. These people will be incorporated as a mode of living already wasted, by-passed; they will be relegated to the status of living refuse. Occupying a position no longer relevant, no longer able to have something to say to white desires for mobility, people of color are a living reminder that everything once useful returns to be immanently useful, but only by being acknowledged as already dead. Blacks are increasingly the main producers of American culture. Yet, so long as their contributions are made within a society which commodifies psychological change, they will have little impact on the structure of American thought. The fact that blacks are the main people making culture simply demonstrates that the production of cultural difference is a thing of the past. The usefulness of their cultural productions rests solely in the reminder that culture no longer exists.

In America, to be satisfied with being oneself is to live at the scene of a fatal crime which could occur at any moment. The Western self rushes to get away yet takes her own policing functions with her. The emphasis is on speed. Not only does the individual want to get from here to there quickly, she also longs for the opportunity to conclude that she was never in the place vacated to begin with. What is hoped for are instantaneous transitions that cover enormous distances. In the end, it is not the experience of movement which is desired, but the obliteration of movement, the obscuring of the fact that one has been altered at all. The individual attempts to get away from positions feared to announce death. However, there is little about that death which the person wants to understand. No relationship is sought out between one death and other deaths, one position and other positions, one self and other selves.

To engage in actual movement and to observe that movement necessitate the following considerations:

¶ What does my change have to do with other people and their changes?

¶ What significance will these changes have for others and, thus, for me?

¶ Why did I change instead of stay the same? and;

¶ What has the place/self/image I'm moving toward have to do with the one I'm moving out of?

The emphasis on speed seeks to make such considerations and questioning unnecessary. At the moment of departure, the individual has already arrived at the new site, is already within it. Accordingly, adaptation to the new "environs" makes such questioning an archaic exercise. There are simply no relationships between the former and the present, and no need to derive any. But precisely because such questioning is not conducted, the itch for another vacation or abandonment is soon felt, and another life is soon wasted.

✿ 34 ✿

WESTERN MAN HAS TRADITIONALLY SOUGHT GUARANTEED success in his relationships with nature, success in his attempts to dominate it. He attempts to find some conceptual means for converting his relative weakness in face of a vast array of external forces into the possibility of his triumph over them.

First, the relationship between man and nature is conceptualized as a game of moves and counter-moves where the exterior world is forced to take man into consideration. Relationships between man and nature, between men, become antagonistic competitions where the initial contrasts between weak and strong (moves and players) are not sufficient to ensure a progressive and consistent harnessing of the exterior world: The weak can outmaneuver the strong, and, then, as strong, can be outmaneuvered by weaker forces in an infinite displacement of clear victory. Anyone who has observed the power struggles within "disturbed" families, where one or more members are either schizophrenic or severely depressed (i.e., "weak"), realizes that the "weak" are often strongest. Through their weakness they are able to exert control over the total operations of the family's life. The strong are never strong enough to always be in control.

As Serres outlines the logical dimensions of this power game in his review of the fable on the wolf and the lamb, "(a person) must maximize (his position) in an absolute fashion; in such a way that there may not exist, that one may not conceive a majorant to a maximum and a minorant to a minimum." "One must transform force into factual necessity and obedience, into an inevitable law... one no longer hesitates to invoke science in the realm of law, power, and politics...because science has already pointed the way to a winning strategy... the reason of the strongest is reason itself " (1979: 269, 276).

The maximum positions have shifted. The reason of God has given way to the reason of the death of God. This, in turn, has given way to the reason of disinterested science, then to the reason of the death of science. Progressively, death itself has become the maximum and minimum position simultaneously, that insurmountable force or limit which freezes the game into a mere reflection of itself. In the long run, it doesn't matter what position is occupied.

In this scheme, death is no longer a sense of negation or a subverter of definitiveness undermining the stability and recognition of binary categories (e.g., strong/weak; presence/absence; here/there) and enabling them to participate in an infinite series of realignments and manuevers. Death becomes the great homogenizer which renders every

171

game the same game, every player the same player, the boring functionary that keep the ledgers neat and clean. This is a death disinterested in its own death; it neither struggles to survive or do itself in and, thus, pays no attention to what or how it is doing (Taylor 1984).

The contestant which can best employ this death, or even become it, has the best chance of preserving the "intactness" of her identity, of not having to be swayed, moved, or altered by the strategic maneuvers of others. Here, the player plunges ahead thoroughly engrossed in his own self-presentation, oblivious to the particular reactions of others, in fact, thriving off any type of reaction as the guarantee for his need to show what he shows, be who he is. To paraphrase Blanchot (1981), social relationships are conceptualized as instantaneously capable of being defined. Others are usually perceived alternately as either total threats or completely irrelevant. The desire to play with and rearrange thoughts, events, and situations, born out of the imagination of an unprecedented life, is attenuated and forlorn.

Children increasingly conclude that they won't have much of a future. Having seen the full rage of adult life, especially the many inabilities of adults to fully protect them from their fears and anxieties, or nurture their aspirations, children often question the efficacy of exerting attempts to make themselves into anything other than quick money machines or objects of glamour. Each day they are exposed to new ways they could be killed, as much of the knowledge presently generated concerns the dangers, diseases, and madnesses that lurk around every corner. As a maximum/minimum position, death is not that which enables us to comprehend our differences but, instead, is used to civilize them, order them, make them speak values in relationship to their comparison, talk about levels and kinds that stick together and have rights over others.

Unlike the majority of Third World societies, the West tends to see death only as the tragic demise of life rather than as a force within life (Taylor 1984). However, only something that is viewed as already completed, possessed, satiated, or closed can be appropriately viewed as available to demise. The life that the West has feared would be over too soon, too abruptly, is then, in a sense, already dead, over to begin with. Already completed, this life has nothing more to learn or become and simply guards against the immanence of its loss.

In many Third World societies, the fullness of a person's life is not to be found entirely in the place where one gazes upon it. There is a connection with that life and person beyond the history or fate of the corporeal body which articulates it. Therefore, feelings of irrevocable loss when the person is not physically present are rare.

In the West, the fear and impact of loss, actual or potential, is pervasive. Loss is considered the major source of psychological stress. The experience of loss as a result of the illness, death, or separation of significant others is seen as the primary factor in the etiology of psychological dysfunctioning. Whether the disturbing implication of loss stems from the guilt of survival, the fear of independence, or the inability to conceive of oneself as separate from the bonds with an other, the fear or suffering involves a "loss of what has never taken place, of a self-presence which has never been given but only dreamed of, and always already split, repeated, incapable of appearing to itself except in its own disappearance" (Derrida 1976, 112).

Acceptance of death entails the acceptance of an essential purposelessness to the activity of existing, where there is never reason adequate enough for the unequivocable justification of particular modes of thinking about and living that existence, no logic of exclusivity or irrevocable distancing of opposites. Such acceptance entails a radical indifference to the slipperiness and provisionality of attempts to systematize coherent meanings for life experience. Even as the clarity of form and structure fade for individuals in the approach of death, attempts to become oblivious to this loss of clarity too often become last gasp manuevers to believe in clarity by testifying to its negation, i.e., "none of this is really happening"; "I am not really here."

An example of such a last ditch effort to keep every perception clear can be found in the final moments of the Werner Herzog film *Aguirre, Wrath of God,* where a raft containing the emaciated and delirious party of Spanish conquistadors drifts in circles as Indians attack from the shore. A dying soldier whispers, "this is not blood, this is not an arrow," and one could imagine him going on to say, "this is not death."

To be freed from the fear of loss entails circling in the crosscurrents of resignation and acceptance—death is more than it appears to be, yet, it is also just what it is in the moment it arrives. There can be no fancy footwork, no negating its appearance since it already is its own negation, and more. Dispossessed, shameless, and irresponsible, those accepting their dying live on wandering through the unraveling of the events and situations which held them together, cohered them into recognizable entities. At the same time, other designs are woven with the strands now loosened. Life in death, and death in life are propositions no longer perceived as contradictions. Instead, they work at cross-purposes to ensure that a vital difference is maintained, that differences in sense, appearance, enunciation, personhood, location, and becomings continue to be produced. "For the freeing on difference requires thought without contradictions, without dialectics, without negation; thought that accepts divergences; affirmative thought whose instrument is dysjunction; thought of the multiple—of the nomadic and dispersed multiplicity that is not limited or confined by the constraints of similarity" (Foucault, 1977: 18).

Preoccupied with death, the West has understood that it produces a great variety of conceptual, social, and experiential differences. But the orientation to these differences treats them as exceptions rather than the norm. They are to have little impact upon the common sense, the common knowledge of the culture. I am not suggesting that such differences should be incorporated or subsumed by a master discourse which synthesizes all disparate variations. The common itself is to be continuously reinvigorated with the potential inputs from all facets and sectors of a culture. The role of the diversity is precisely to deter the consolidation of any set agenda, principles, meanings, or interpreters in establishing permanently stable guidelines for or readings of common sense. The common is to be kept off guard so that it may be viewed as open to the contributions and uses of everyone. The common is to enable everyone to maintain and/or alter themselves as they imagine. The intent of common sense, its reason for existence is to make sure that no one particular faction or sector of a culture claims it as its own, availing every member of a culture to the possibility of feeling confident in themselves, desirous of being who they are. Common sense is the knowledge open to all. Not only is it open to all to read, understand, and use, but available to shaping by all hands.

The postmodern period is characterized by the normality of the exception—it is the norm for there to be rampant exceptions and for these exceptions to appear openly in public. Because the array of social and behavioral differences is understood as exceptions, the diffusion of messages and influences, although existent, is still highly limited because of Euro-American culture's inability to assert a level of commonality for these differences. Not that these differences are to be reduced to conceptual similarities , but that they are viewed as usable by everyone, and thus, common.

The dominant view in Western thought regards seeing and visual sense as the primary mode of understanding, as reflected in such comments, "I see what you mean" or, "it's all clear now." Western thought has been characterized by an ambivalent relationship between thought and language. On the one hand, the mimetic provides the surest affirmation of the real. But as a sign or stand-in for that which is real, it must be regarded with a permanent suspicion that the mimetic conceals some essential truth or thing unavailable to the senses. The suspicion leads Western cultures to prioritize the activity of producing speech and writing, i.e., meta-communicative procedures for talking about talking, thinking about thinking.

In this recourse to a meta-linguistic level, the ambiguity of thought and communication is seemingly objectified, made into a concrete entity capable of eliciting sustained reflection and analysis by thought itself— an attempt to circumvent the formlessness of thought by systematizing the activity if not the manifestations of thinking and communicating. What something is, then, becomes determined and verified by creative and inductive inquiry. Rather than the creation and communication of ideas being products of the various rhetorical inventions assembled by a culture from the available stock of linguistic and semiotic resources, ideas are viewed as intact and continuous entities fully and verifiably known only through the application of a master discourse. "Knowledge thus suborned by method became not what everyone knew, but what they might know if they employed the critical method that would lead reason from the observation of things to inductive generalization" (Tyler, 1984: 37).

When the common is devalued as a result of the privileging of reason, its ability to cohere, sustain, and intermingle the vast array of feelings, signs, behaviors, and social configurations produced by culture is diminished. The production of exceptions and the commonality of the status, "exception," makes social life appear as a field of disconnected minorities, subcultures, pluralities, and lifestyles functionally operating within common geographical and administrative territories but stripped of a sense of psychological connection. A plethora of possibilities for conceiving and articulating social identity become available. Despite the fact that the individual is presented with vast choices about what she can be, where she can go, and what she can do, these choices are still experienced in a static manner. That is, movement among and living within these choices rarely influence the shape, implications, and experiences of the other available possibilities.

In a city such as New York, you can frequently see interracial couples on the street and the convergence of all ethnicities. It's no big deal. Still, most viewers attend to these couplings in a special way. The display generates a surplus of meaning. However, the surplus is rarely used by the viewer as an influence on her own thinking and behavior. The event remains a permanent curiosity which neither surprises or informs. Without depth to most viewers, the coupling addresses only the superficial curiosities, becomes a sign of the incorporation of the marginal into the normative visual and social field, and is accepted only as long as it remains marginal and aloof to lives resuscitated by the endless consumption of the exceptional and not by the breadth of their potential versatility.

The obsession with the certainty and continuity of human advancement, with certainty in winning, is to be obsessed with death. Yet, the game of winning eventually implodes. Technological advancement deployed to prolong human existence has partially culminated in the capacity to destroy all human existence through nuclear, viral, and genetic warfare. The postmodern message is: we must now save ourselves by reducing differences capable of producing "dangerous" antagonisms. The human community must become more alike if we are to survive and prevent a global holocaust. We must monitor (as effectively as possible) sexual practices, the raising of families, the training, education, and movement of bodies. All singular positions and conditions characterizing actual or potential relationships between ourselves and the exterior world collapse into each other. Here, Western notions of death legitimate an assault upon the differences which not only characterize our relationships with each other, but with death itself. The Western refusal to accept the murkiness and disorder of lived reality means that notions of death are deprived of intelligence and, instead, are ploddingly confined to being the arbiter and culmination of everything temporal.

Distorting themselves to cushion the impact of death, Western selves have unconsciously hoped that they might find a cure for the distortions in death. The West is convinced that only death will be the last remaining unknown phenomenon. Everything else is up for grabs, fair game, capable of being dictated to, transformed, and made over. That which resists is then viewed as an evil or darkness from which we must rescue our nature and hope. Whatever a person is not doing becomes dangerous to whatever she is doing, threatens to contaminate or imperil all that is lived for. And what is lived for has historically been either a particular and glorious position in the universe of the non-living, an eternal life or nothingness, or earthly experiences capable of abnegating the reality of death.

The obsession with death stops Western individuals from being themselves, stops them from permitting the resiliency and malleability that death implicitly provides them, a malleability that might enable individuals to understand their mortality and, thus, the provisional and tentative qualities of nature and the shape of human existence. To acknowledge death is to acknowledge the freedom we have as individuals and a culture to invent who we are, to change or recreate the convention through which we determine who we are and where we are going. Western man, the great inventor of technologies, consistently shies away from accepting the fact that she invents herself.

In the West, forms of culture and selfhood, and conventions structuring thought and behavior, are seen to be the end products of the synthesis of diverse experiences, trial and error, struggle and blood that has finally arrived at the truth or ideal form of social life. Much has been tried. If we don't necessarily conclude that ideal states of existence have been reached, then, at least, we tend to believe that we have a clear idea about what we must do to get there. In a culture which conceives its conventions as the products of hard-fought struggle and the supremacy of reason, there is a limited tolerance for exceptions or variations, unless endless variation itself becomes the predominant norm, where everybody is the same by virtue of how varied each person's life becomes.

Whatever its shape, convention survives because of the failure of any challenge to it rather than persisting beyond the strength or necessity of the challenge. Thus, all challenges must be turned into failures. The unconventional represents, then, an individual or group's inability to conform and is conceptualized as a problem of their efforts rather than as deficiencies in the conventions themselves. Any therapeutic or reform agent who tries to get an individual to normalize herself must at the same time implicitly highlight the individual's isolation and peculiarity, bring to her attention that she has a problem. It is likely that she will come to recognize her own pathology. She sees the adherence to convention as cure. As dysfunctional, marginal, and in need of rehabilitation, the individual who acts in unconventional ways tends to reframe her challenge as neurosis, sees herself as lacking the legitimacy or mental health to challenge effectively. Perhaps unwilling to relinquish the problematic behavior, she makes a life out of the pathology, holds onto it tenaciously. But framed and viewed as pathological, the behaviors are unable to effectively challenge and undo existing norms.

In much of the Black World, the conventions of cultures are not sufficient in themselves for specifying how an individual is to live. To be wife, mother, father, grandmother, etc.— even though the cultural definitions of these roles specify a range of appropriate actions—must be charged with actions and thoughts that threaten to tear apart the ties a person has with her roles and the ties that exist among discrete social actors. Only in this fashion can the conventions be known and affirmed in their power to exist despite and in face of individual variation (Wagner, 1981). If the conventions cannot be actively challenged, picked at, or threatened, they are of little value as conventions, i.e., means for organizing and understanding social life Even if these challenges or ruptures produce anguish, difficulty, isolation, and emotional pain, the viability of normative social relationships are being confirmed in the process.

In much of the Third World, there still exists boldness, impetuousness, and risk in the ways people live out their adventures and enthusiasms (Wagner, 1981). By trying to consciously and deliberately assert her radical uniqueness from and irrelevance to others, the individual will fail on some level. The more wild the attempt, the more elegant the failure and, thus, the more an essential humanity and similarity to others is revealed. A moral order is created despite the attempts not to create one. As a result, a moral order becomes worthy of the utmost seriousness and respect.

Part of the West's difficulty in acting out this impetuousness stems from the institutionalized conflation of convention with the standardization of linguistic, expressive, and social norms. Such standardization of discourse reflects the West's pervasive anxiety about its capacity to utilize its interpretive possibilities intelligently and widely. Emphasis has traditionally been placed on attempts to make interpretation unnecessary by converting convention into an unequivocable reference or set of procedures for constituting and exchanging sense in everyday life. Convention as specific procedures or standards for making sense obscures the reasons for why conventions are important in the first place. Rather than overcoming, denying, or compensating for the murkiness and ambiguity of lived reality, conventions are most usefully viewed as provisional strategies for enabling individuals to conclude some sense in their relationships, some interrelationship between their individual and collective lives. Conventions were to be viewed, not as stolid prescriptions for individual action, but as facilitators of opportunistic and ad hoc social behavior.

Conventions exist to:

¶ Produce conceptions of the multiple events, turbulences, and irruptions occurring in any social context;

¶ Produce vehicles for communicating such conceptions;

¶ Foster a group's willingness to initiate, maintain, or reframe potential and existent social affiliations;

¶ Create, exchange, disseminate, and interpret understandings, intentions, reports, observations, and evaluations;

¶ Enable an individual or group to roughly estimate the implications entailed by thinking, acting, and feeling in a given way and;

¶ Interrelate a corpus of existent and potential behaviors and provide them with significance, by defining and elaborating their meaning in terms of every other behavior.

In other words, the role of convention is to sustain a notion of human community. Such sustenance necessitates:

¶ Provisions for a surplus of interpretive activity regarding anything produced or done by that community;

¶ Beliefs in the justifiability of any explanation or behavior rather than adherence to a particular justification and;

¶ Manifestations of expression, thought, and behavior that exceed the capacity of any regulatory system to fully apprehend them as the necessary preconditions and legitimation of the social norms constructed.

Whether or not the intelligibility of social interaction is provided by the linguistic vehicles used to operate within them, any comprehension of these interactions still must be negotiated and recognized in the process of interaction itself. In attributing definitiveness or clarity exclusively to linguistic or semiotic vehicles, the communication system, or the social norms, the competence necessary for individuals to produce meaning for their lived experiences is mitigated. No matter how clearly a relationship is defined, there will still be many ambiguities. Instead of seeing such ambiguities as opportunities to steer an interpersonal relationship in a variety of directions, individuals regard them as sources of anxiety and dread.

According to Baudrillard (1983), standardization attempts to "fabricate the neutral," engender an indifferent application of sense to all phenomena. This neutrality is familiar to us all in the form of science and technology. At the same time, Baudrillard reminds us, we probably hope for some turbulence and unpredictability, some special meaning designed and determined for the peculiarities of our individual life situations—a delerium, an unprecedented coming together of events, situations, and voices. As Western reason attempts to "resolve all fatality into causality or probability," notions of chance and randomness must be constructed where there are no possibilities of meaningful interconnections between conceptual forms and significance, conventions and cultures, situations and events, people and people outside of clearly stated cause-effect relationships.

Every thing which is to have meaning has it for a specifiable, measurable, and predictable reason. Chance and randomness become the definitive proof of the supremacy of Western reason, the justification for standardization, and the grounds for the dismissal of Third World fatalism. Instead of connoting an open-ended world, or the variegated and unpredictable circulation of bodies and objects, chance is employed as the proof of Western rationalism. The only order and the only viable convention is that of reason, and the disorder of experiences, appearances, and events is only accidental, never conventional.

The cosmologies of non-Western peoples have repeatedly demonstrated intersections among lives and occurrences that proceed in a predetermined fashion. Although frequently criticized for their lack of resolve and initiative, non-Western peoples know how to take advantage of their lack of efficiency in scheduling, planning, and developing their everyday lives. It has been said that their sheer lack of expectations for things to work out means that little will work out. However, despite the best intentions, procedures, and expectations, Western life is full of accidents, frustrations, and missed opportunities. Unlike the Western orientation, these "accidents" and "breakdowns" rarely produce an accumulation of stress, frustration, or depression in Third World contexts. Non-Western peoples tend to foresee the perpetual immanence of the accident and are prepared to achieve some sense of personal homeostasis when confronted with it. There is little psychological stress in African cultures despite the individual and social hardships. If something happens, it happens; if not, the flow of life continues. Events will still transpire, surprises will still take place that one can enjoy and develop. There is little use to implicate the fallabilities of oneself or others; no need to worry that there is something an individual could have done to set the course in any other way.

The shaping of Western personality, its acceptance or rejection by others, and its world-views and confirmations, occurs in a seemingly prophetic manner. If a person is worried about rejection, separation, or illness, they will tend to act in ways that guarantee these things. In the locus of every individual existence are examples of discrete events that mutually uncover, reveal, or explain each other even though they are separated by years and incalculable psychological distances. These are conventional processes, yet, analysts of any kind would be hard-pressed to understand them with unequivocable logics or explanations.

"We would like there to be chance, nonsense, hence innocence, and for the gods to continue to play dice with the universe, but we prefer that there be everywhere sovereignty, cruelty, total interconnection, we prefer events to be the radical consequence of thought. We like one and prefer the other." (Baudrillard, 1983: 289)

Baudrillard is saying that the conventions we use to understand life embody notions of life that are dystonic to the ways we prefer to see ourselves living. On the horizon is the possibility of cause and effect reversing themselves, even of life and death exchanging places, set against each other simply to imply the other. Signs of certainty connote the impossibility of any summation and indications of ambiguity resound strikingly precise and clear. Everything is upended, surprised. Nothing is what it should be and, thus, is what it is; the start is the end, the end is the beginning.

Traditionally, the West has addressed the problem of death by making life and death invisible to each other, by creating a world of pure appearance and disappearance disconnected from any temporal reference and retrievable in any space. The parameters of humanity are altered to accomodate the obsession; life disappears to make the obsession go away.

In his review of alterations in the technological paradigms of the twentieth century, Yves Stourdze (1980) emphasizes that the tendency to produce an optimal, standardized level of functioning in individuals threatens to make the idea of humanness permanently vague and obsolete. In the genetic-electronic society, individual identity is deconstructed and reconstituted in potentially infinite ways within and across transmission systems that invalidate distance and physical separation. A social body is created through the consumption of a space/time that has no reference or equivalent in reality. The subsequent diversity and unpredictability of the interconnections between various sign and information systems will be so immense as to render unequivocable readings impossible. Human adaptation will increasingly necessitate manipulation of an exclusively semiotic universe. Simulations of multiplex levels of social being will be calculated algebraically. Finally, individuals will be detached from a consensually defined human community viewed as limiting the capacity of the individual to incessantly and rapidly transform the parameters of selfhood. Stourdze thinks the attempt to standardize the conventions necessary for the sustenance of human communities permanently alters the humanness of the community which these conventions were designed and implemented to sustain.

Most of what we know about intelligence, cognition, and social behavior is on the verge of being simulated by non-human, artificial entities and operations. More than ever, Western cultures must now explicitly deal with their attitudes, fears, and orientations about death. They must confront the provisionality of lived experience, the permanently equivocal relationships that exist between the shape, nature, and direction of lived experience, and the timing, predictability, nature, or onset of death.

Individuals must deal with these issues in order to invent humanity once again, to exceed their ideas about themselves, and to extend themselves to those people they have wasted and denied. The preoccupation with death led Western cultures to close ranks, protect and defend images of themselves they could not renew but only intensify, rearrange, magnify, condense, or simulate. These cultures must now invent the ability to recognize and love themselves through learning, borrowing, and incorporating what they can from wherever they can in a fashion nurturing of the peoples borrowed from. To live life with the primary focus being the attempt to keep death away, to postpone or hasten it, is to live for death and neglect what can be done in life.

To live, an individual must go where she doesn't belong and is not expected to survive. She must attempt the impossible connections. Selves who are seemingly the most self-destructive frequently live the longest. Those who cautiously and diligently spin a web of protection and fitness often are the first to go.

The thrust of contemporary medicine and therapeutics, although seemingly encouraging people to sustain their health and increase their fitness, still attempts to do combat with death and generate knowledges about how to postpone or delay it. Rarely, do these therapeutics posit a wide range of conceivable strategies for living — strategies that ultimately must risk death. As demonstrated in the Kuranko narratives of Zaire, what is most important in living, what is most moral, fulfilling, harmonious, and just, must often be sought through means and orientations not only inimical to social convention but to the continuation of life itself (Jackson, 1982).

Traditionally, Africans have sought out death, sought out the means to go to it and return from it. The African has been unwilling to be passive in face of it; she has not turned from it for she knows that this confrontation is the only means whereby she can strive to make God "adapt to the arrangement which follows her desire to live" (Zahan, 1979: 154). In Kane's (1963) book, *Ambiguous Adventure,* a young Diallobe man studying in Paris testifies: "It seems to me, for example, that in the country of the Diallobe man is closer to death. He lives on more familiar terms with it. His existence acquires from it something like an aftermath of authenticity. Down there, there existed between death and myself an intimacy, made up at the same time of my terror and my expectation. Whereas here death has become a stranger to me. Everything combats it, drives it back from men's bodies and minds. I forget about it. When I search for it in my thought, I see only a dried-up sentiment, an abstract eventuality, scarcely more disagreeable for me than for my insurance company." (149)

Michael Taussig, a social anthropologist, has written extensively on the issues of terror and healing in Third World cultures. In his article on colonial practices of torture in the Putamayo Indians of Columbia, he warns that the West must learn to dispense with the need to see danger and catastrophe everywhere, because this need leads us to choreograph intricate displays of that catastrophe and danger. The West sees horror where there is no horror, death where there is no death. It is time to pay attention to a different story, or more importantly, stop trying to make people of color recite the story we have been telling ourselves all along. No longer should America take advantage of the Black World's intimacy with death by making it experience the deaths we in the West shun and refuse to become familiar with.

Much has been made here about the importance of diversity and the saliency of cultural difference. The emphasis on such plurality is not to be viewed as fodder for new revolutionary political programs or the architecture of an ideal society. Such views would render static the ebb and flow that exists in simultaneous recognitions of the strangeness and familiarity in those persons and experience which are different. I am not proposing the "United Nations of all peoples in the world co-existing in essential harmony," metaphors that populate liberal imaginations. The livelihood of social plurality is the mutable tensions plurality generates.

All recognitions and understandings are provisional and curious. No social arrangement stabilizes itself in an economy of negotiated valences accorded to intergroup exchanges, where all participants consensually agree to accord specific values to each other's contributions. Multiraciality depends upon a perpetual antagonism and uncertainty over the effects of interaction. The purpose of social policies related to interracial matters are most effectively geared to maximizing points of interaction rather than harmonizing, balancing, or equillibrating the distribution of bodies, resources, and territories. Whites must come to see such interaction as indispensable to a re-emerged sense of daring and vitality, to their aspirations for irresponsibility and wantonness, since appeals to morality and conscience simply stimulate the idea that confusion and ambiguity are states to be overcome or rationally dealt with.

6

Calling Upon Each Other:
Race as an Occasion
For Cultural Nurturance

✿ 36 ✿

REFERENCE IS MADE IN THE PREVIOUS CHAPTER TO RECOUPING
the ability to invent self and culture. What is to be invented
are scattered and heterogeneous domains within the present
confines of an individual's life which suggest various and,
usually, contradictory possibilities for an ongoing existence.

Here, a person would be capable of simultaneously thinking about how to act under a number of very different conditions She would prepare herself for multiple futures. The purpose of the plurality is not simply to cover all the conceivable bases, to make a home for imaginations drenched in ambivalence, or make all futures look the same. Rather, the focus is on altering the present situation where individual and social imaginations are always suspected of harboring a repressed underside, where one image is known to conceal another which, in turn, reveals/conceals another. The heterogeneity I have in mind simply concedes that individuals are capable of many contrasting thoughts and behaviors. Whatever cohesiveness is attained is more in the form of a travelogue rather than self-reflection.

The future can not only be conceived as the eventual necessity of having to solve a series of social problems or accommodating/repressing marginalized social bodies. Paralleling efforts at problem-solving, individuals must imagine and, to a limited extent, act as if all futures were viable. It is important to imagine a world in which everyone was black, no one was black, there were no white/black contacts, or where sociality was predominantly characterized by interracial interaction.

Even though Lévi-Strauss' (1976) game of chance view of diachrony as a succession of associative chains linking inventions in one culture to another has been roundly criticized as idealizing the function of cultural diversity, it is important to keep in mind one of his points: The viability of cultural productions and inventions is rarely concluded by cultures in advance. There are no specific limitations concerning what practices will enhance or detract from a culture's functioning prior to that culture's actual use and experimentation with these processes. The sheer existence of a knowledge system does not legitimate the system's applicability to the people who create it. Rather, history is a sequence both of problems addressed and left unaddressed; knowledges acquired and discarded; social characteristics that are loved yet given up, while aspects of self and society that are criticized are often maintained. Even when cultures possess notions about the procedures necessary for ideal or optimal functioning, they continue to produce forms and engage in practices which appear to detract from the attainment of these optimal states. Within any culture, many different agendas and futures compete for individual and collective attention. Options are to be kept open.

The value of cultural forms foreign to one particular culture lies in their ability to foster and provide a language for the restlessness of individuals or groups existing within that culture. Exposure to this diversity provides the momentum necessary for the culture to continue being itself by exceeding itself. The diversity of forms and inputs does not provide the materials for the creation of ideal or superordinate individuals or societies. Since pleasure and satisfaction can be derived from many behaviors and emotions, what this plurality looks like or should look like is largely contingent upon the specific time and place in which it occurs.

In Bakhtin's formulation of the "transgredient," the self understands what it is by turning toward some other self (Todorov 1984). Here, the other is the surplus of vision

195

necessary for the self to realize a sense of completion, to have a sense of self. If the other is merely identified with, fused with, or viewed as a co-participant in a larger conception which becomes the real locus of identity, self-completion is not possible. The other ceases to be someone with whom the self exchanges, talks, engages, and disengages. The pulling away from another person is as important in the process of creative understanding as is the joining with them. A sense of interaction is maintained only as long as interactants acknowledge themselves as different and the difference is not construed as prohibitive of the interaction. Therefore, the function of the interaction is not to callibrate, regulate, or homogenize the effects or outcomes but to cultivate, albeit, redistribute the difference. Each person is altered, but not for the purpose of equalizing or synthesizing each person's impact on the other.

The oscillation of separateness and togetherness is a dynamic yet to be imagined in the context of American race relations. Unable to position themselves at the cusp of the convergence between commonality and separateness, whites tend to invoke their own invented attributions of black life as the impediment to commonality. In turn, they use the absence of commonality as a way to criticize any black desire for limited cultural or psychological separateness. The message to the Black community is: we can't really be together but don't act as if we can't be together, that is, don't appear to be together or cohesive amongst yourselves.

Inculcated in an ethos of self-sufficiency, whites continue to be troubled and anxious about the apparent solidarity of blacks— a solidarity that is threatening because it seemingly resists all attempts to differentiate blacks from conditions thought to contribute to their continued perceptions of collective racial interest. That is, not even class stratification substantially diminishes the significance race has to black people.

This is not to say that such solidarity always assumes useful forms. Although there are substantial traditions of communality in black cultures, elements of a negative solidarity have a propensity to interweave themselves into these traditions. Unity is achieved as often by a mutual limiting and undercutting of the growth and movement of individuals as it is by contributions enhancing of each individual's interests. The attitude is: if not everyone can get ahead, then no one will get ahead. If no one is getting ahead, then it is especially important that no one recognize that it is their own behavior which contributes to this inability. External others and conditions must be blamed. Even if these others and conditions are responsible for the group's hardships or define the conditions under which the group must exist, to do nothing but blame becomes self-defeating. hen the collective efforts of the group are devoted to assigning fault, the group's efforts, instead of raising a people's consciousness, are more likely to waste it.

Despite lengthy histories of both interaction and separation, pervasive anxieties about the white man continue to exist among black men. Within an international context of gender politics, they are thrust into various domains oriented around individual competition and, thus, comparison, as vehicles for attaining a sense of self-completion. It is easy to both excuse and criticize black men for their often exaggerated displays of a bankrupt authoritarianism and consumptions of phallocentric frameworks for self-evaluation. Yet, neither the excuses or criticisms diminish a rampant and desperate hunger for the trappings of self-respect imposed on them from childhood. Power becomes the cure for their failed aspirations.

To gain and maintain power is not desired for the force it provides creative activity. Rather, it is the means for resisting being made nothing. But even with power, the individual is not much more than nothing, because the maintenance of power necessitates that the person diminish the risk-taking which is an inherent part of the enlivening of imagination. Without the imagination, a person might as well be nothing. There are nothings that live in luxury and nothings who live in destitution.

Black and white men rarely find themselves able to sit down with each other in any capacity because they must always suspect that any mutuality will be construed by the other, and thus by themselves, as a loss of position, power, and self. Black women, because of the dual nature of their subjugation and their long history of turning to each other with the urgent need for reciprocity, tend to exhibit less anxiety in interracial contacts, especially women who experienced a high degree of separateness from the white world during their childhoods. Not having to constantly deal with the white man enables them to deal with him with greater assuredness and creativity. Frequent calls for black solidarity, like "driven needs to make it in the white world," can be motivated just as much from the fear blacks may have of feeling insufficient in relation to whites as much as it can

198

genuinely reflect self-respect and political commitment. Both separateness and togetherness should be viewed as inextricable aspects of the development of white and black consciousness.

Despite the fact that black solidarity and communality are often illusory or products of ritualistic citation rather than real political coordination, black individuals rarely see or conceptualize themselves as alone. Additionally, they are seen by whites as having recourse to a level of explanation that reframes individual uncertainty or deprecation as an aspect of a collective condition which all black individuals share. Even though feelings of dependency, incompetence, and self-doubt may be extreme among black individuals, whites continue to be suspicious of blacks because they tend to believe that blacks don't really care about independence, competence, or self-confidence. Whites often think that blacks don't need to be self-sufficient; there is and always will be other blacks around who will be obligated to feed, clothe, or shelter individuals having a hard time. Despite the fallacy of such perceptions, much of the thrust of the welfare system could be viewed as an attempt by the state to attenuate both the desire and capacity of black kinship systems to provide communal support. Independent and alone, the white self in dire conditions will have no one to turn to and so must relate to others in terms of gaining advantage over them and use that advantage to instill a restraining guilt in those with whom there has been a selective and calculated sharing of information and resources.

As was indicated earlier, there are many examples of the social resiliency of African-American culture and the

199

ways the collective aspirations of blacks took precedence over the fulfillment of individual desires. But this is not the solidarity that troubles white minds. The historical inability of whites to relate reciprocally with broad collective configurations or distinct cultural domains is translated into a pervasive fear that a supposed black orientation toward acting in collective concert will minimize the efficacy of all white social and individual activity. In interracial contacts, whites fear that it is never a one on one situation, but one white against a black other who acts as an agent for an entire people. The absurdity of this proposition points out not only the alienation and insecurity of white identity but also reveals a recurrent jealousy and envy, where whites feel that no matter what direction an individual black life takes, its mistakes, tragedies, joys, accidents, and stupidities are always imbued with a larger purpose unavailable to white existence.

This fear and jealousy is why most whites are anxious to get rid of race as an explicit means for looking at and talking about the organization of American society. Additionally, this is why American society is anxious to multiply the number of communicable and salient social designations so that everyone, despite historical and cultural convergences, political and economic advantage, will be apprehendable solely in terms specific to their supposed singularity.The engineering of a seamless society of an infinite number of minorities is especially important as blacks continue to appeal to a sense of human dignity, liberation, and solace.

Euro-American social practice tends to approach the

cultural differences of others by attempting to eradicate the difference altogether. According to Lévi-Strauss, this has been the crux of global westernization. Whites move to vitiate the forcefulness of a black solidarity which whites themselves, for the most part, have fabricated. What unity and concerted action does exist is not in the forms in which whites fear it exists. The solidarity is both a sign of continued degradation and strength; whether it would exist in the absence of racism is an open question. By removing the vestiges of degradation, African-Americans also risk eliminating the images through which they have maintained a semblance of uniqueness and vitality as a minority people, even though these images have not normalized their presence within Euro-American culture.

It is important to keep in mind that racism is an operation that is also applied by whites to themselves. On the one hand, racism acts to restrict the black other and her experience to a prescribed and limited domain of operation. On the other, it seeks to cultivate a certain blindness and deafness in the white self, attenuating any feelings of guilt or incompleteness that might emanate from such a diminution of the senses making sense. The white self now primarily hears only highly differentiated voices and looks upon only highly stylized and rarified visual appearances. The white self tries to resolve her anxieties about racial differences by attuning herself to differences which she considers more different than those of race. What is common or comprehensible ceases to signify.

In a universe of multiple discourses and parallel worlds, there is no univocal authority or rectifying force.

Each person must live in her own time and agenda, where only the exceptional and hyperindividual attain visibility and recognition, and then only for a moment as the difference can only be noted and not really used. What life is like for large social bodies is hardly discernable, especially as the former political languages are distrusted or considered violations of where the substance of freedom actually lies. No one and everyone are responsible for the important decisions. Unable to conceptualize life in terms of a "we-ness," whites increasingly view blackness as an archaic and expendable distinction.

Whites have generally considered blacks in broad social terms—as race, community, or bloc. In emerging policies of deracination, the white invention is now retracted: racial differences are absorbed in cognitive frameworks that privilege singular events, psyches, and social practices.

The differences are absorbed to solidify the advantage of Euro-American culture over every other. Such hyper-individualism conceals a fundamental homogenization and consolidation of diverse political and economic functions around the world under the rubric of Western administration. To affirm that there is no single, overarching Truth is merely to recuperate it inversely through its proclaimed absence. Rather than positing the truthfulness and applicability of many diverse truths and knowledges, a multiplicity of truths is deployed to connote the basic evidence for the absence of any guidance or revolutionary prospects. As an executive working in a multinational corporation in Abidjan told me, "the world has set its own course, and there is little we can do about it." The prevalent postmodern attitude is:

if everything is so interconnected and contingent upon realities which a person has no access to, what, in the long run, can really be done about influencing any situation confronted? There are just too many factors to consider.

The nature of truth and reality is not reconceptualized as a series of specific and limited effects shaped by particular discursive strategies Rather, the multiplicity of truths in the postmodern era is construed as the inverted legitimation of the continued existence of a single, uncontroverted epistemology which some cultural, political, or corporate sector will still have to define. The appropriate function of heterogeneity is to posit understandings that are never final and always provisional. Yet, the diversity of lives, significations, codes, images, knowledges, and realities now simply amplifies interminable uncertainty instead of maximizing opportunities for concluding provisional certainties. Postmodern diversity reduces all articulations and modes of living to a just boredom and expendable equality rather than maximizing opportunities for description, individual variation, and social imagination. Thus, plurality becomes the incipient paradigm for a revised domination that controls through the exhaustion individuals increasingly feel as the product of their ineffectual, inordinate, and monotonous choosing. Still trapped in the either/or dichotomies of planning for one's future, the postmodern individual must now, more than ever, make the right choice.

Individuals need the courage and diligence to live out contradictory versions of themselves, where the white individual can alternate between total immersion in and dismissal of the Black World, and all points in between. Again, the point is not the attainment of a balance or synthesis of black and white worlds. Conversely, such intersections would continuously throw each world off balance, off guard, and enable individuals to engage and retreat, accept and deplore. Mutual understanding is to be used to challenge each world into new questions and uncertainties, enable each to enjoin the other as developmental forces without anyone being subsumed by the other. At all times, whites and blacks will risk mutual derision, rejection, suspicion, and aloofness, yet, any movement and change in their respective positions will indicate that something important has been contributed and learned. To engage and pull away—each process is vital to the other.

AS WE LIVE, WE LIVE NOT ONLY FOR THE STEPS TAKEN, CHOICES made, territories occupied, or ideas and bodies embraced. We live also for another corresponding, possible world, another space brought to life precisely by our choice not to live it. Every time we choose, follow, or create one particular course, we posit and realize other alternative courses as well. Others exist to enunciate and embody these possible worlds, to acknowledge the incompleteness and provisionality of the life course we pursue. Because of this tentativeness, and because we know that there are other ways to live and courses to follow, people desire contact and interaction with others, some mingling of worlds. The image or conception of the Other is neither completely definitive or fully experienced by the self and, as such, draws her into it, absorbs both the beginning and end of the life she recognizes as hers. It is through the Other that the self understands the possibilities of authoring her own existence, surprising herself with her own capacities.

I would extend Deleuze's (1984) discussion on the structure of perversion to encompass the nature of racism. In perversion, Deleuze suggests that the body and self of the Other is annulled. In the Other, there is no resemblance or familiarity to the existing self, only endoublement or mimicry. When perceived by this existing self, the Other is not there, is invisible. The self thinks: "she, the Other, is just like me; therefore, she isn't really there, visible to my perception; since I see only differences, there is nothing here to see." In this annulment of the Other, a sense of a life beyond that presently lived and a future of alternative, possible worlds is cancelled. A world without an Other is a world of no future possibilities. Everything is reduced to utter necessity, crisis, optimum performance, urgency, and the auto-legitimation of power. All differences are dissolved, and what is desired becomes the sheer repetition of survival. The responsibility of that survival is increasingly turned over to an array of support systems, i.e., artificial intelligences, therapies, consumptions, and technologies which enable individuals to deny that they have any role or input in social life. Once again, the image of impotence and inefficacy predominates.

It is common knowledge that, in many respects, America has lost its sense of the future. We do what we can to get ahead, because getting ahead is what it takes to survive. There are no grand visions. Outside of removing governmental interventions thought to be obstacles to getting ahead, there is little sense of purpose. The free enterprise system is to be reinvigorated so that more people can make money. But where this takes us as a people is far from clear, as we jump from crisis to crisis. We know that ahead lies great uncertainties and dangers. But we tend to see what lies ahead as simply not there, as something that will simply happen, occur when the time comes.

In a racial framework, there is a strong tendency in America to view blacks in their blackness as simply not there, as neither suggesting or representing positive, alarming, or possible futures. Their presence is reduced to a fact of everyday life neither precipitating fear or curiosity. The blackness of blacks, that which designates their otherness for whites, is now predominantly viewed and comprehended as a piece of social data, an expression of a social problem, a reminder of the absence and irrelevance of once significant moral values, or an aspect of cultural entertainment. Rarely does this blackness challenge and open up how whites conceive and think about their living, how they make choices, how they will be selves. Until this input and this mingling of possibilities is used and accepted, the passions of racial animosity will smoulder and seethe.

❧ 38 ❧

LEERY OF CALLS TO EITHER PROGRAMMATIC RIGOR OR MORAL vigilance, I cannot offer systematic plans for the rehabilitation of white people. Neither conscience, self-interest, or guilt will undo the persistence of racialist effects, even if the deracination policies of the eighties pretend to sound the death knell for discrimination of any sort. What a strategy of racial counter-politics should be is contingent upon what forms are implemented to minimize the fluid and reciprocal interactions of whiteness and blackness In this era of resumed silence, where the blackness of blacks is viewed as insignificant to the living, work, and educational situations of black people, a certain discursive explicitness appears warranted. Race-talk, talk about race and cultural difference, is important as long as such talk occurs interracially as well as within the interior of each racial or cultural group. Too often, an awkward comfort in black-white relationships is achieved only by silencing overt reference to the distinctions, whether they be cultural or personal. At other times, interracial intersection occurs solely for making reference to such distinctions, for discussing the raciality of the interaction and, thus, white and black never move beyond acknowledgement or exploration of the impediments to do something else with each other.

In some areas of the country, there is a resurgence of interracial marriage and love relationships. The motivations for this resurgence are multifarious and complex. At times these relationships are fraught with material interests and aspirations for social advancement that characterize amorous relationships of any kind. Here, such materialism is foregrounded because frequently people refuse to believe that there would be any other reason for blacks and whites to come together in this manner. Advantage is not one-sided. Affiliations with blacks are often construed as signs of status among young whites, especially those working in the cultural sectors where the influences of Afro-America are most clearly evident.

Whether interracial affiliations are sought for a certain status is not the point. Even if the motivations are demonstrated to be sincere, their believability will always be challenged or questioned by some simply because the affiliation exists. Although overt intolerance and discrimination against such coupling has greatly diminished in the past two decades, an array of micropolitical intimidations, scrutinies, and anxieties continue to envelope these relationships, often promoting heightened degrees of self-consciousness in the couple which debilitate, or at least, distract.

Biracial couples often compensate for these difficulties by over-zealous declarations about how wonderful and important the relationship is, transforming the relationship into a mission or political agenda. The couple makes itself out to be more than it is. At times, it is difficult for the couple to sort out what problems are intrinsic to them as individuals and as a couple from the difficulties generated by the punitive attitudes of others external to the relationship. By downplaying externally produced difficulties, the couple increases its vulnerability to them. Often a division of labor is structured where remedial or "diplomatic" work for the relationship is racially territorialized. In other words, each member of the couple "works on" family, associates, and friends of the same race and become the sole recipient of their evaluations, supports and criticisms. Rarely does the couple conjointly assume the responsibility of dealing with both white and black worlds as they impact upon the relationship.

Although it is important for biracial support networks to assist couples in defending against the harrassments leveled against them and to celebrate the virtues of such couplings, they might also assist in enabling couples to be active in designing various public "presentations" of their coupledom to different social contexts. Instead of hiding from the world and from substantial social exposure, strategies could be developed to enhance the visibility of such affiliations so they may affect a decrease in public scrutiny and everyday "clinical" observation. Additionally, such support networks should be oriented toward mitigating the guilt often incumbent in biracial relationships and conceive of ways for groups of biracial couples to appear in and intersect with social life which elicit an explicit articulation of a full range of racial attitudes from both whites and blacks. Such might occur by couples occasionally traversing public spaces in "packs" and cultivating, through repeated frequenting, places where biracial couples or single individuals desirous of such affiliations can interact and jointly participate in a variety of political, educational, or recreational activities that spill out into segregated sectors.

The biracial couple is placed in a larger social context where it must often fight for its life. Emphasis could be placed on how to use the couple form or a social network of couples to undermine the micro-technologies of intimidation and intervene strategically into the psychology of the larger social body precisely by using these vehicles where blacks and whites find their greatest intimacy and, also, most profound cultural clashes. Couples have always existed for functions and purposes beyond their own particular interests. So it may be viable to find ways to extend the use of this already existent institution of convergence, no matter how small or limited it may be, to constitute incipient forms of a broader nexus or organization, rather than searching for ways to convene and organize intentional groupings.

✿ 39 ✿

IN AFRICAN AMERICAN CULTURE, REFERENCE IS OFTEN MADE to "calling upon" emotional, spiritual, and cognitive resources that are viewed as part of a tradition of personal, familial, or collective experience. Such traditions are not readily defined or codified, partly because they are perceived to be either marginal or at odds with conventional practices for thinking about living. Such resources may never be "called upon," yet it is important that individuals maintain the capacity to do so in any circumstance. More than a simple call for help or invocation of invisible powers, the request for guidance is directed to enabling the individual to look at her current situation in a different way. The act is an indication of the person's strength and confidence rather than confusion or weakness. One does not call upon such resources to problem-solve or adapt, but to act in ways that exceed the demands or expectations of the context, to go beyond what is overtly made known in order to invent unforeseen opportunities.

Precisely how these resources are identified vary greatly with African American, but despite the fuzziness of the denotative aspects of these resources, there is usually broad and common agreement on just what is being called upon. Rather than rescue or clarification, the call involves the capacity for wisdom and for new behavioral or spiritual possibilities—the same possibilities Deleuze (1984) has indicated are entailed in the desire for otherness. The need for the supplement of these resources, instead of indicating that something is missing or deficient in the character who invokes them, signifies that the person is prepared to accept new responsibilities, and has demonstrated courage in foregoing the satisfactions of what is familiar in order to activate new challenges.

The ability to call is as important as the calling itself. When asked to "break" the knowledge down or to codify its contributions, African Americans usually refer to ancestral perspectives, an alignment of the individual with a rearticulation of collective intelligence which frames the individual as both a manifestation of a culture's ongoingness and a critical burgeoning of a new application of culture, i.e., an individual instance of the culture venturing into psychological domains where it hasn't gone before.

In way of summary, these resources might be called acceptable procedures for inventiveness, since what is eventually known is neither old or new. In many respects, the act of calling upon these resources becomes one of the most important acts of African American cultural affirmation. Accordingly, this practice is to be considerate of the implications such calling entails for the resources called upon. When perceived as the wisdom, experiences, or interventions of ancestors, any calling must be assessed in terms of the consequences such calling has for the ancestors. The "caller" neither wants to deplete, antagonize, overextend, or misapply these resources for they are not an eternal and static wellspring that is applicable or viable in the same, continuous ways. The nature of the calling, in turn, must nurture the resources, must heighten their creative powers, and enhance their resiliency.

The knowledge, events, or courses of action produced by this reference are to be cooperatively produced. Never is this knowledge perceived as capable of being possessed or used by a single person alone; it is never to be accumulated or hoarded. The individual turns away from herself, externalizes both the dilemma and the insight. Knowledge becomes an act of social association; what transpires is never totally apprehendable in the confines of the person who calls. Others, known and unknown, are enjoined in the calling; there is no readily identifiable or circumscribed territory of effects, neither ancestor or invoker know quite what will happen as a result.

In all these aspects, the act of calling may be an appropriate metaphor for a conceptualization of mutually-nurturing interracial exchanges. In the variation of historical and cultural experiences played out within a shared national framework, American whites and blacks could be a resource for each other, called upon, not for precise prescriptions, answers, or models of living, but as collaborations thinking about everyday living through heterogeneous perspectives and modes of assessment. Just as the individual who invokes must keep in mind the possible implications for the resources called upon, such collaborations would, by definition, avoid parasitism. Such mutual calling would proceed out of perceptions of adequacy and strength, and a desire to exceed the known and the functional.

If such mutual callings are to be realized, whites and blacks must attribute fundamental differences to each other. The affirmation of differences need not question or cloud fundamental similarities in the basic areas of human competence, affect, and sociality, but reach for experiences and expressions of human desires which exceed what has been known. The affirmation of the common is de-emphasized only so that the nature of that common can be expanded, reshaped, and empowered.

No individual, society, or culture can be complete in its own right. And contributions from the outside are not intended to compensate or make-up for deficiencies. With this perspective, there is no need for comparison; white and black exist for each other to suggest opportunities and possibilities of action, thinking, and feeling that go beyond each culture's proven capacity to survive and adapt to a wide range of contexts and circumstances. The designations, "white" and "black," have always been excessive. That is, they have connoted aspects of human existence which have transcended mere survival or the functional contingencies of human behavior. Sense can be made of such designations only if they are maintained as excessive, as connotations that motivate an individual, living as a member of a particular society, to exceed the roles and sensibilities in which her existence is inscribed, where she always moves to be more than what she recognizes herself to be. "White" and "black" were terms invented to absorb anything said about them, to contain all possibilities.

Inevitably, if whites and blacks are to call upon each other as supplementary resources, the question comes up concerning what each group will call that which is to be called upon. What is it in the experience, heritage, and social cognition of African Americans that whites could use; how will this be defined and what will it be called. In African American tradition, the resources have no precise designation. They are open-ended, ambiguous, and diffuse. The act of calling is prioritized over the identification of that which is called upon. In fact, the knowledge to be used cannot be precisely identified because the calling itself is a unique collaboration. None of the parties know quite what to expect, and the reciprocity is maintained exactly because there is no precise definition. These resources, strengths, ideas, and exchanges can only be labeled with provisional designations. One calls them anything at all only to acknowledge that such a process of collaboration is being attempted, just to indicate that something is taking place.

Participants in this process need not worry excessively about how they designate, invoke, or communicate with these resources. They must only keep in mind the fact that both blacks and whites historically prefer not to be seen or called certain things. I emphasize the inherent resiliency of the labelling process because whites are reluctant to discuss blackness at all, let alone attribute to blacks a range of characteristics and experiences that could complement what they know and experience as whites. Part of this reluctance is understandable. Whites today prefer not to see themselves as racists or hear the designation applied to their way of talking. Uncertain as to which of their views of blacks will be construed as racist, whites become taciturn about expressing any views at all, or articulate, in either serious, ironical, or joking manners, the views blacks themselves have informed whites they expect from them.

So in some ways, it is safer to regurgitate the familiar views of blacks as either substantially oppressed, welfare cheats, or superlative producers of culture, than to articulate convictions about aspects of blackness worth learning from or paying attention to. Additionally, as a result of blacks making the claim that any knowledge about blackness should be generated by blacks themselves, whites have been deterred from substantial observations and investigations of African American concerns.

Given the invidious history of white research, the insistence of blacks on generating their own knowledge and conducting their own research is understandable. Yet, I believe such a position of racial exclusivity is also dangerous for (1) the ongoing cultivation of a distinct African American cultural base within the United States, and (2) a potential diminution of institutional racism. A possible return to the old trappings of overt racialist discourse must be risked in order for both whites and blacks to see something valuable in the experiences and cognition of the other, especially in an era where deracination is used as a significant vehicle for racial oppression. When too much is made of the white man by blacks, the white man, indeed, becomes too much to handle. Benign neglect was an attitude more appropriately prescribed for blacks rather than for whites; that is, many blacks are able to pay attention to themselves only by focusing on what the white man is doing to them.

Whether the content of what whites see as valuable in African American culture is the stuff of romanticized projections or split off attributions is not as a significant factor as the sheer experience of turning to blacks for something that exceeds doing what is necessary to survive. Blacks will have to increasingly act out a hard-won confidence in their knowledge of whites to assure themselves that participation in such a reciprocal pedagogy does not inevitably mean that they will be taken advantage of once again. Obviously their own use of white culture for their own purposes has not substantially endangered the continuity of white domination; there is, conversely, little reason to expect that whites learning from blacks will severely endanger black survival or political aspirations. What is truly disarming for whites is not proclamations of moral vigilance or revolutionary ardor in black discourse, but the increasing confidence displayed by some blacks in their curiosity and willingness to listen to and use various aspects of Euro-American culture to extend the parameters of their operations as black individuals. The diminution of racial defensiveness becomes the strongest mechanism for defending the integrity of blackness.

All mutual contributions, as products of called upon and daring collaborations, can only be guessed at or speculated about beforehand. Therefore, there are no specified limits about what can be said, what the other can be called. Blacks and whites may have to initiate a period where they say a great deal about each other to each other. Antagonism as well as cooperation will be produced, offense as well as tenderness. The goal of these encounters should not be reconciliation or social harmony but mutual disruption—disruption of what is familiar to both. I doubt that America will experience any profound transition in the nature of race relations without first experiencing a process where affectual responses are intensified. In order to maximize the degree of mutual respect and nurturance, animosity and rage have to be expected. Yet, the explicit mistakes and stumbling, the wrong moves and lack of optimal behavioral performances, may constitute a significant improvement over the current state, where both whites and blacks frequently pretend that attention to racial matters is a thing best relegated to the past.

Instead of being quick to condemn each other for the formulations made about each other, whites and blacks must act in ways to develop confidence in these interracial exchanges and feel comfortable about who they are. This confidence is obtained only if both whites and blacks expect each other to make mistakes, to be frequently off-base, or outrageously inept. In this way, whatever mutually acknowledged benefits derive from such collaboration might be met with genuine surprise instead of being scrutinized for their inevitable or intrinsic limitations. What is suggested here is neither a political program or a definitive answer to the demise of racism. It is a way of thinking about a necessary attitude, a way of taking black and white fears, attractions, hostilities, exhaustions, and possibilities somewhere else.

In Camara Laye's book *The Radiance of the King,* a European man has come to Africa with hopes of being taken into the service of a King, who is widely touted as possessing a personal magnificence unparalleled anywhere on the continent. The European has no idea about what he could offer, except his good will. Yet, the desire for this opportunity consumes him. Even upon discovering the king to be a frail adolescent does not deter the European from his pursuit. Aided by a wily and thoroughly ingratiating beggar, who lives off of the European's meager resources, the white man experiences countless absurd hardships in an arduous journey to wait for the king's next appearance in a particularly remote part of the monarch's realm. Reduced to years of utter lassitude while awaiting the elusive king, the European discovers that the beggar had sold him as a stud to service the harem of an old *maribout* during re- peated nights of unconsciousness. Cognizant of this fact only moments before the king's long-awaited arrival, the European, thoroughly shamed, is confronted with having to relinquish his longheld desire just before it is to be fulfilled.

Despite his feelings of complete debasement, the European is, nonetheless, beckoned by the king and envel- oped in his love. Nothing is exchanged, calculated, owned, or stolen. There is only "your hunger which calls to my hunger." In the embrace between the black king and his white "servant" is a love for a spirit that has not yet had the opportunity to continue its vital growth and a love for a desire that finds itself completely alone and dispossessed of everything it once was confident in. In a historical period where whites and blacks may soon have little to say to each other as whites and blacks, the courage to express this love for a familiar spirit, whose own ascendancy comforts the recognition of unfamiliar deaths, may be the only force capable of taking blacks and whites through all the attempted unbecomings.

In recent years, more white people seek out the knowledge, styles, and attitudes of their black counterparts. For the most part, the intersection with blackness in not born out of a confusion of identity, self-disgust, or pretentions to hipness. Although critical of the legacies and intellectual habits of whiteness, this burgeoning white character doesn't despise itself for being white. Rather, she feels a desire to come to terms with her whiteness, so as to dismantle lingering impediments to the development of self-confidence and, thus, a capacity to be daring, provocative, and generous.

Without many affirmative notions about what it means, the whiteness of whites tends to be something defined by non-white others as a body of advantages and limitations. Increasingly, white "seekers" see that the only way to comes to terms with their whiteness is to provide it with some positive impetus, some affirmative value. This impetus comes exactly from a willingness to lose what is already lost, that is, to adamantly insist upon learning from those people who were, in the past, defined by whiteness as the objects of its condescending, patronizing, and imposed teachings. By reversing the "pedagogical" relationship on which whiteness has historically depended for its self-recognition and sustenance, the development of a "new" whiteness enjoins itself to the nurturance of the black other's capacity to teach. As soon as whiteness attempts to consolidate some advantage over blackness, it undermines the very relationship which contributes to a renewed confidence and comprehension of itself.

What is important here is that the attempt to recoup a sensibility and knowledge of whiteness is based on attempts to forget it, stretch it, or rearrange it through the incorporation of the thoughts, passions, and styles of Third World cultures both in and out of America. These attempts provide a vehicle for whites to participate in a solidarity with each other based on their own specific and singular attempts to burst open the confines of how they have permitted themselves to be known. They provide whites with an additional vehicle through which to engage with each other in a kind of sociality long moribund, having been converted into a psychology of people climbing on and over each other's backs in attempts to get ahead and undermine the efforts of others. Here, the restructuration of white cultural identity itself becomes the constitution of culture and a space of common sociality for white Americans. It is a culture where African-American history becomes American history, and African-American thought and spirit, America's thought and spirit.

References

Aaron, D.
1983 "The 'Inky' Curse: Miscegenation in the white American literary imagination." *Social Science Information* 22, 2: 169–190.

Abrahams, R. D.
1970 *Positively Black*. Englewood Cliffs, N.J.: Prentice-Hall.

Abrahams, R. D. and Szwed, J.
1983 *After Africa*. New Haven: Yale University Press.

Alleyne, M. C.
1980 *Comparative Afro-American: a historical-comparative study of English-based Afro-American dialects of the New World*. Ann Arbor: Karoma.

Alverson, H.
1978 *Mind in the Heart of Darkness*. New Haven: Yale University Press.

References

Amer, M. and Isaacs, L.
1978 "Determinants and Behavioral Consequences of Psychological Modernity." *American Sociological Review* 43: 316–43.

Anyanwu, K. C.
1976 "Scientific Attitudes and African Human Experience." *Thought and Practice* 3, 2: 141–153.

Apostel, L.
1981 *African Philosophy: myth or reality*. Brussels: Story-Scientia.

Apostle, R. A.; Gluck, C. Y.; Piazza, T., Suelzle, M.
1983 *The Anatomy of Racial Attitudes*. Berkeley: University of California Press.

Ardener, E. W.
1981 "Some Outstanding Events in the Analysis of Events." In Le Cron Foster, S. H. Brandes (eds.), *Symbol as Sense: new approaches to the analysis of meaning*. New York: Academic Press.

Aschenbrenner, J.
1974 "Community and Variations in Black Family Structure." In D. Shimkin et al. (eds.), *The Extended Family in Black Societies*. The Hague: Mouton.

Austin, A. D.
1984 *African Muslims in Antebellum America* New York: Garland Publishing.

Bailey, F. G.
1983 *The Tactical Use of Passion: an essay on power, reason, and reality*. Ithaca, N.Y.: Cornell University Press.

Baker, D.G.
1983 *Race, Ethnicity, and Power: a comparative study*. London: Routledge and Kegan Paul.

222

Balandier, G.
1970 *The Sociology of Black Africa.* New York: Praeger.

Banton, M.
1977 *The Idea of Race.* London: Tavistock.

1983 *Racial and Ethnic Competition.* Cambridge: Cambridge University Press.

Barnes-Harden, A.
1984 "Cross-cultural Understanding Among Peoples of African Descent: African continuities as a unifying agent." *Journal of Black Studies,* 15, 1:31-41.

Barthes, R.
1974 *S/Z: an essay.* New York: Hill and Wang.

Baudrillard, J.
1983 "Totality or Reversible Immanence: beyond the uncertainty principle." *Social Research* 47: 273-95.

1983 *Simulations.* New York: Semiotext(e) Foreign Agents Series.

Bauer, D. F. and Hinnant, J.
1980 "Normal and Revolutionary Divination: a Kuhnian approach to African traditional thought." In I. Karp and C.S. Bird (eds.), *African Systems of Thought.* Bloomington, Ind.: Indiana University Press.

Baugh, J.
1983 *Black Street Speech.* Austin: University of Texas Press.

Baughman, E. E.
1971 *Black American: a psychological analysis.* New York: Academic Press.

References

Berreman, G. D.
1972 "Race, Caste, and Other Invidious Distinctions in Social Stratification." *Race* 13,8.

Berry, J. W.
1976 *Human Ecology and Cognitive Styles: comparative studies in cultural and psychological adaptation.* New York: Wiley.

Binet, J.
1984 "Development: transfer of technologies; transfer of culture." *Diogenes* 126: 19-38.

Blanchot, M.
1981 *The Gaze of Orpheus.* Barrytown, N.Y.: Station Hill Press.

Blauer, R.
1972 *Racial Oppression in America.* New York: Harper and Row.

Bloor, D.
1976 *Knowledge and Social Imagery.* London: Routledge and Kegan Paul.

Blumer, H. and Duster, T.
1981 "Theories of Race and Social Action." *Sociological Theories: Race and Colonialism.* Paris: UNESCO.

Blyden, E.
1967 *Christianity, Islam, and the Negro Race.* Edinburgh: Oxford University Press.

Bourdieu, P.
1977 *Outline for a Theory of Practice.* Cambridge: Cambridge University Press.

Boykins, A. W.; Franklin, A. J. and Yates, J. F.
1979 *Research Directions of Black Psychologists.* New York: Russell Sage.

Buxton, J.
1972 *Religion and Healing in Mandari*. Oxford: Oxford University Press.

Calinescu, M.
1983 "From the One to the Many: pluralism in today's thought." In I. Hassan and S. Hassan (eds.), *Innovation/Renovation: new perspectives in the humanities*. Madison: University of Wisconsin Press.

Campbell, B. A.
1980 "The Interaction of Race and Socioeconomic Status in the Development of Political Attitudes." *Social Science Quarterly* 80: 651-658.

Castells, M.
1983 *The City and the Grassroots: a cross-cultural theory of urban social movements*. London: Edwin Arnorld.

Caton, C. E
1966 "On the Global Structure of the Epistemic Qualifications of Things Said in English." *Foundations of Language* 2: 37-66.

1981 "Stainaker on Pragmatic Presupposition." In P. Cole (ed.), *Radical Pragmatics*. New York: Academic Press.

Christmas, J. J.
1973 "Self Concept and Attitudes." In K.S. Miller and R. M. Dreger (eds.), *Comparative Studies of Whites and Blacks in the United States*. Norwood, N.J.: ABLEX.

Clark, C. X., Nobles, W.; McGee, D. P.; and Weems, L. X.
1975 "Vodoo or IQ: an introduction to African psychology." *The Journal of Black Psychology* I, 2: 56-65.

Cohen, R.
1978 "Ethnicity: problem and form in anthropology." *Annual Review of Anthropoplogy* 7: 309-404.

References

Cohen, W.
1980 *The French Encounter with Africa: white responses to blacks 1530-1880.* Bloomington, Ind.: Indiana University Press.

Cole, M. and Scribner, S.
1974 *Culture and Thought.* New York: Wiley.

Collins, S. M.
1983 "The Making of the Black Middle Class." *Social Problems* 30, 4: 360-382.

Comaroff, J. L. and Simm, R.
1981 *Rules and Processes: the cultural logic of dispute in an African context.* Chicago: Chicago University Press.

Crocker, J. C.
1977 "The Social Function of Rhetorical Forms." In J. D. Sapir and J. C. Crocker (eds.), *The Social Use of Metaphor: essays on the anthropology of rhetoric.* Philadelphia: University of Pennsylvania Press.

Curtin, P. D.
1964 *The Image of Africa.* Madison: University of Wisconsin Press.

Deleuze, G.
1984 "Michel Tournier and the World without Others" *Economy and Society* 13, 1.

Derrida, J.
1976 *On Grammatology.* Baltimore: Johns Hopkins University Press.

1977a "Signature Event Context." *Glyph* 1: 172-197.

1977b "Limited inc abc" *Glyph* 2: 162-2S4

1979 "Living On: Borderlines." In H. Bloom et al (eds.), *Deconstruction and Criticism.* New York: Seabury Press.

1981a *Dissemination*. Chicago: University of Chicago Press.

1981b *Positions*. Chicago: University of Chicago Press.

Doob, L. W.
1971 *Patterning of Time*. New Haven: Yale University Press.

1975 *Pathways to People*. New Haven: Yale University Press.

1983 *Personality, Power, and Authority*. Westport, Ct.: Greenwood Press.

Dominguez, J.
1976 *Capital Flows in Minority Areas*. Lexington, Mass.: Lexington Books.

Drake, St. Clair
1982 "Diaspora Studies and Pan Africanism." In J. E. Harris (ed.), *Global Dimensions of the African Diaspora*. Washington, D.C.: Howard University Press.

Dreitzel, H. P.
1981 "The Socialization of Nature: Western attitudes toward body and emotions." In P. Heelas and A. Lock (eds.), *Indigenous Psychologies: the anthropology of the self*. New York: Academic Press.

Du Bois, W. E. B.
1961 *The Souls of Black Folk*. New York: Fawcett Books.

Duvingnaud, J.
1962 *Change at Shebika*. New York: Pantheon.

Eco, U.
1976 *A Theory of Semiotics*. Bloomington, Ind.: Indiana University Press.

References

1984 *Semiotics and the Philosophy of Language.* Bloomington, Ind.: Indiana Unversity Press.

Elias, N.
1978 *The Civilizing Process.* London: Basil Blackwell.

English, R. H.
1974 "Beyond Pathology: research and theoretical perspectives on black families." In L. Gary (ed.), *Social Research in the Black Community: selected issues and priorities.* Washington, D. C.: Howard University Institute for Urban Affairs and Research.

Epstein, A. L.
1978 *Ethos and Identity.* London: Tavistock.

Fabian, J.
1971 *Jamaa: A Charismatic Movement in Katanga.* Evanston, Ill.: Northwestern University Press.

1983 *Time and the Other: how anthropology makes its object.* New York: Columbia Unversity Press.

Fanon, F.
1965 *A Dying Colonialism.* London: Pelican.

1967 *Toward an African Revolution.* Monthly Review Press.

1968 *The Wretched of the Earth.* New York: Grove Press.

Farrakhan, L.
1973 *Three Speeches.* New York: East.

Fernandez, J. W.
1972 "Fang Representation Under Acculturation." In P. D. Curtin (ed.), *Africa and the West: intellectual responses to Western culture.* Madison: University of Wisconsin Press.

1974 "The Mission of Metaphor in Expressive Culture." *Current Anthropology.* 15: 119-145.

1978 "African Religious Movements." *Annual Review of Anthropology* 7: 195-234.

1980 "Edification by Puzzlement." In I. Karp and C. S. Bird (eds.), *African Systems of Thought.* Bloomington, Ind.: Indiana University Press.

Folb, E.
1980 *Runnin' Down Some Lines.* Cambridge, Mass.: Harvard University Press.

Foucault, M.
1970 *The Order of Things: An Archeology of the Human Sciences.* Pantheon.

1972 *The Archeology of Knowledge.* New York: Pantheon.

1977a *Discipline and Punish.* New York: Pantheon.

1977b *Language, Counter-Memory, Practice.* Ithaca, N.Y.: Cornell University Press

1980 *Power/Knowledge.* New York: Pantheon.

Frank, A. G.
1975 *On Capitalist Underdevelopment.* New York: Oxford University Press.

Frederickson, G. M.
1972 *Black Image in the White Mind: the debate on Afro-American character and destiny 1817-1914.* New York: Harper.

Freeman, R.
1976 *The Black Elite.* New York: McGraw-Hill.

References

Friedman, J. B.
1981 *The Monstrous Races in Medieval Art and Thought*. Cambridge, Mass.: Harvard University Press.

Fusfeld, D. R. and Bates, T.
1984 *The Political Economy of the Urban Ghetto*. Carbondale, Ill.: Southern Illinois University Press.

Geertz, C.
1973 *The Interpretation of Culture: selected essays*. New York: Basic Books.

1983 *Local Knowledge*. New York: Basic Books.

1984 "Anti Anti-Relativism." *American Anthropologist* 86, 2: 263-278.

Genovese, E.
1972 *In Red and Black: Marxist explorations in Southern and Afro-American history*. New York: Vintage.

Gladwin, T. and Saidin, A.
1980 *Slaves of the White Myth: the psychology of neocolonialism*. Atlantic Highlands, N.J.: Humanities Press.

Glenn, E. S.
1974 "The Thory of Meaning and Some Cognitive Considerations for the Analysis of Differences Between Cultures." *Communication and Cognition* 7, 3/4: 407-437.

Goffman, E.
1969 *Strategic Interaction*. Philadelphia: University of Pennsylvania Press.

1974 *Frame Analysis: an essay on the organization of experience*. New York: Harper and Row.

1981 *Forms of Talk*. Philadelphia: University of Pennsylvania Press.

Gordon, V. (ed.)
1979 *Lectures: Black Scholars on Black Issues*. Washington, D. C.: University Press of America.

Greenberg, S. B.
1980 *Race and State in Capitalist Development*. New Haven: Yale University Press.

Grier, W. and Cobbs, P.
1969 *Black Rage*. New York: Basic Books.

Grosscup, B.
1978 "The Racial Rationale: constructing a theory of international power." *World Affairs* 140, 4: 284-303.

Gumperz, J.
1971 *Language in Social Groups*. Palo Alto: Stanford Univ. Press.

1982 *Discourse Strategies*. New York: Cambridge University Press.

Gutman, H. G.
1976 *The Black Family in Slavery and Freedom 1750-1925*. New York: Pantheon.

Gwaltney, J. L.
1980 *Drylongso: a self-portrait of Black America*. New York: Random House.

Hamilton, D. L. and Bishop, G. D.
1976 "Attitudinal and Behavioral Effects on Initial Integration of White Suburban Neighborhoods." *Journal of Social Issues* 32: 47-67.

References

Hannerz, U.
  1968 "The Rhetoric of Soul: Identification in Negro Society." *Race* 9:453-465.

  1972 "The Study of Afro-American Cultural Dynamics.." *Southwestern Journal of Anthropology* 27: 181-200.

  1975 "Research in the Black Ghetto: A review of the sixties." In R. D. Abrahams and J. Szwed (eds.), *Discovering Afro-America.*

Harms, R. W.
  1983 "Diagonal Narratives in African History." *The American Historical Review* 88, 4: 809-834.

Harris, P. and Heelas, P.
  1979 "Cognitive Processes of Collective Representation" *European Journal of Sociology* 20: 211-241.

Hauser, S. T.
  1971 *Black and White Identity Formation.* New York: John Wiley and Sons.

Hawkins, D. J.
  1980 "Social Structure as Metatheory: implications for race relations theory and research." In C. B. Marrett and C. Leggen (eds.), *Research in Race Relations.* Volume 2 Greenwich, Ct: Jai Press.

Heelas, P. and Lock, A. (eds.)
  1981 *Indigenous Psychologies: the anthropology of the self.* London: Academic.

Herskovitz, M. J.
  1958 *The Myth of the Negro Past.* Boston: Beacon Press.

Hill, H.
1984 "Race and Ethnicity in Organized Labor: the historical sources of resistance to affirmative action." *Journal of Intergroup Relations* 12,4: 4-59.

Hirsch, A. R.
1983 *Making the Second Ghetto: race and housing in Chicago 1940-1960*. New York: Cambridge University Press.

Hoetink, H.
1973 *Slavery and Race Relations in the Americas: comparative studies on their nature and nexus*. New York: Harper.

1979 "The Cultural Links." In M. E. Crahan and F . Knight (eds.), *Africa in the Caribbean: the legacies of a link*. Baltimore: Johns Hopkins University Press.

Hountondji, P.
1983 *African Philosophy*. Bloomington, Ind.: Indiana University Press.

Huggins, N. I.; Kilson, M., and Fox, D.
1971 *Key Issues in the Afro-American Experience*. New York: Harcourt Brace Jovanovich.

Hurston, Z. N.
1979 *The Sanctified Church*. Berkeley: Turtle Island.

Hymes, D.
1974 *Foundations in Sociolinguistics*. Philadelphia: University of Pennsylvania Press.

Jackson, G. G.
1980 "The African Genesis of the Black Perspective in Helping." In R. Jones (ed.), *Black Psychology*. New York: Harper and Row.

References

Jackson, M.
1982 *Allegories of the Wilderness: ethics and ambiguity in Kuranko narratives*. Bloomington, Ind.: Indiana University Press.

Jahoda, G.
1970 "Supernatural Beliefs and Changing Cognitive Structures Among Ghanaian University Students." *Journal of Cross-Cultural Psychology* 1: 115-130.

1975 "Applying Cross-Cultural Psychology to the Third World." In J. W. Berry and W. S. Lonner (eds.), *Applied Cross-Cultural Psychology*. Amsterdam: Swets and Zeitlinger.

Jenkins, A.
1982 *The Psychology of the Afro-American*. New York: Pergamon.

Johnson, L. A.
1981 "Cultural Relativism and 'Parity of Esteem': a test case." In V. I. Bickley and J. P. Puthenparampil (eds.), *Cultural Relations in the Global Community: problems and prospects*. New Dehli: Abhinav Publications.

Jones, R. S. and Dzidzienyo, A.
1976 "Social Structure and Racial Ideologies in New York." Conference on the African Mind in the New World. Rutgers University.

Jules-Rosette, B.
1978 "The Veil of Objectivity: prophecy, divination, and social inquiry." *American Anthropologist* 80, 3: 549-570.

1979 *New Religions of Africa*. Norwood, N. J.: ABLEX.

Kane, C. H.
1963 *Ambiguous Adventure*. London: Heinmann.

Kaufan, R. L.
1983 "A Structural Decomposition of Black-White Earning Differentials." *American Journal of Sociology* 89, 3: 58-611

Kavolis, V.
1984 "On the Self-Person Differentiation: universal categories of civilization and their diverse contents." In V. Kavolis (ed.), *Designs of Selfhood*. Cranbury, N. J.: Associated University Presses.

Kilson, D. de B.
1976 "Afro-American Social Structure 1790-1970." In M. L. Kilson and R. Rotberg (eds.), *The African Diaspora*. Cambridge, Mass.: Harvard University Press.

Kiple, K. F. and King, V. H.
1981 *Another Dimension to the African Diaspora: diet, disease, and racism*. New York: Cambridge University Press.

Kochman, T.
1981 *Black and White Styles in Conflict*. Chicago: University of Chicago Press.

Kovel, J.
1970 *White Racism*. New York: Vintage.

Kristeva, J.
1975 "The System and the Speaking Subject." In T. Sebeok (ed.), *The Tell-Tale Sign*. Lisse, The Netherlands: Peter De Ridder Press.

1980 *Desire in Language*. New York: Columbia University Press.

Kunene, M.
1981 *Anthem of the Decades: A Zulu epic dedicated to the women of Africa*. London: Heinemann.

References

Kuper, L.
1981 "The Theory of the Plural Society, Race, and Conquest." *Sociological Theories: Race and Colonialism* Paris: UNESCO.

Kuyk, B. M.
1983 "The African Derivation of Black Fraternal Orders in the United States." *Comparative Studies in Society and History.* 25, 4: 559–592.

Labov, W.
1972 *Language in the Inner City: studies in Black English vernacular.* Philadelphia: Unversity of Pennsylvania Press.

Laye, C.
1965 *The Radiance of the King.* London: Fontana.

Leenhardt, M.
1979 *Do Kamo: Person and Myth in the Melanesian World.* Chicago: University of Chicago Press.

Legesse, A.
1973 *Gada: three approaches to the study of African society.* New York: Free Press.

Lerone, B.
1970 *The Challenge of Blackness.* Atlanta: Institute of the Black World.

Levine, L.W.
1977 *Black Culture and Black Consciousness: Afro-American folk thought from slavery to freedom.* New York: Oxford University Press.

Lévi-Strauss, C.
1976 *Structural Anthropology.* vol 2. New York: Basic Books.

Lloyd, B. and Gay, J. (eds.)
1981 *Universals of Human Thought: some African evidence.* Cambridge: Cambridge University Press.

Louche, C.
1982 "Open Conflict and the Dynamics of Intergroup Negotiation." In H. Tajfel (ed.), *Social Identity and Intergroup Relations.* New York: Cambridge University Press.

Lynch, H. R. ed.
1971 *Black Spokesman: selected published writings of Edward Wilmont Blyden.* New York: Humanities Press.

Lyotard, J. F.
1981 *The Postmodern Condition: a report on knowledge.* Minneapolis: University of Minnesota Press.

MacGaffey, W.
1981 "African Ideology and Belief." *African Studies Review* 24, 2/3: 64-98.

Marable, M.
1980 *From the Grassroots: essays toward Afro-American liberation.* South End Press.

Marazzi, C.
1978 "Money and the Global Order." *Zerowork* 1.

Maruyama, M.
1978 "Endogenous Research and Polyocular Anthropology." In R. Hollman and S. A. Arutinunov (eds.), *Perspectives in Ethnicity.* The Hague: Mouton.

Mattelart, A.; Delcourt, X.; and Mattelart, M.
1984 *International Image Markets. in search of alternative perspectives.* London: Comedia.

References

McAdoo, H. P.
1981 *Black Families*. Beverley Hills: Sage Publications.

McCulloch, J.
1983 *Black Soul, White Artifact*. New York: Cambridge University Press.

Miers, S. and Kopytof, M. (eds.)
1977 *Slavery in Africa: historical and anthropological perspectives*. Madison: University of Wisconsin Press.

Mintz, S. W. and Price, R.
1976 *An Anthropological Approach to the Afro-American Past: A Caribbean Perspectve*. Philadelphia: Institute for the Study of Human Issues.

Mithun, J. S.
1983 "The Role of the Family in Acculturation and Assimilation in America: a psychocultural dimension." In W. C. McCready (ed.), *Culture, Ethnicity, and Identity*. New York: Academic Press.

Moscovici, S.
1980 "The Proper Use of Polemics." *Yale French Studies* 58.

Mudimbe, V. Y.
1983 "African Philosophy as an Ideological Practice: the case of French speaking Africa." *African Studies Review* 26: 266-317.

Mutiso, G. C. M.
1976 "African Perceptions of the Ideas of Freedom and Revolution." *Thought and Practice* 3, 2: 127-135.

Negri, T.
1980 "Domination and Sabotage." *Semiotext(e)* 3, 3: 33–51.

Noack, P.
1983 "Crisis Instead of Revolution: on the instrumental change of social innovation. In I. Hassan and S. Hassan (eds.), *Innovation/ Renovation: new perspectives on the humanities*. Madison: University of Wisconsin Press.

Nobles, W. W.
1974 "African Root and American Fruit: The Black Family" *Journal of Social and Behavioral Sciences*, 20: 52-64.

1980 "African Philosophy: Foundations for A Black Psychology." In R. Jones (ed.), *Black Psychology*. Second edition. New York: Harper and Row.

Nobles, W. W. and Goddard, J.
1977 "Consciousness, Adaptability and Coping Strategies: socioeconomic characteristics and ecological issues in black families." *Western Journal of Black Studies* 2: 105-113.

Nunberg, G.
1981 "Validating Pragmatic Explanations." In P. Cole (ed.), *Radical Pragmatics*. New York: Academic Press.

Okere, T.
1983 *African Philosophy: a historico-hermeneutical investigation of the conditions of its possibility*. Lanham, Md.: University Press of America.

Owusu, M.
1978 "Ethnography of Africa: the usefulness of the useless." *American Anthropologist* 80, 2: 310-334.

Patterson, O.
1977 *Ethnic Chauvinism: the reactionary pulse*. New York: Stein and Day.

References

1982 *Slavery and Social Death.* Cambridge, Mass.: Harvard University Press.

Pescatello, A. M.
1977 "The Afro-American in Historical Perspective." In A. M. Pescatello (ed.), *Old Roots in New Lands: historical and anthropological perspectives on Black experiences in the Americas.* Westport, Ct.: Greenwood Press.

Pettrigrew, T.
1964 *A Profile of the Negro American.* Princeton: Van Nostrand.

1981 "Race and Class in the 1980's: an interactive view." *Daedalus* 110, 2: 233-256.

Price, R.
1979 *Maroon Societies: rebel slave communities in the Americas.* Baltimore: Johns Hopkins University Press.

Rabinow, P.
1982 "Masked I Go Forward: reflections on the modern subject." In J. Ruby (ed.), *A Crack in the Mirror.* Philadelphia: University of Pennsylvania Press

Reeves, F.
1983 *British Racial Discourse: A study of British political discourse about race and race related matters.* Cambridge: Cambridge University Press.

Reich, M.
1981 *Racial Inequality.* Princeton: Princeton University Press.

Rex, J.
1981 "Racial Relations and Minority Groups: some convergences." *International Social Science Journal* 33, 2: 351–373.

1983 *Race Relations in Sociological Theory.* second edition. London: Routledge and Kegan Paul.

Rosaldo, M. Z.
1980 *Knowledge and Passion: Ilongot notions of self and social life.* Cambridge: Cambridge University Press.

1984 "Toward an Anthropology of Self and Feeling." In R. A. Shweder and R. A. Le Vine (eds.), *Cultural Theory: essays of mind, self, and emotion.* New York: Cambridge University Press.

Rose, T. L.
1981 "Cognitive and Dyadic Processes in Intergroup Contact." In D. L. Hamilton (ed.), *Cognitive Processes in Stereotyping and Intergroup Behavior.* Hillside, N.J.: Lawrence Erlbaum Associates.

Rosenau, J. N.
1984 "A Pre-Theory Revisited: world politics in an era of cascading interdependence." *International Studies Quarterly* 28, 3: 245-305.

Riesman, P.
1979 *Freedom in Fulani Social Life.* Chicago: University of Chicago Press.

Ryan, M. T.
1981 "Assimilating New Worlds in the Sixteenth and Seventeeth Centuries." *Comparative Studies in Society and History.* 23, 4: 519-538.

Sanders, R.
1978 *Lost Tribes and Promised Lands: the origin of American racism.* Boston: Little, Brown and Company.

Sandywell, B.; Silverman, D.; Roche, M.; and Philipson, M.
1975 *Problems of Reflexivity and Dialectics in Sociological Inquiry.* London: Routledge and Kegan Paul.

References

Sattler, J. M.
1970 "Racial 'Experimenter Effects' in Experimentation, Testing, Interviewing, and Psychotherapy." *Psychological Bulletin* 73: 137-160.

Schneider, D. M.
1976 "Notes Toward a Theory of Culture." In K. Basso and H. Selby (eds.) *Meaning in Anthropology*. Albuquerque: University of New Mexico Press.

Scholte, B.
1981 "Cultural Anthropology and the Paradigm Concept." In L. Graham, W. Lepenies, W. and P. Weingart (eds.), *Functions and Uses of Disciplinary History*. volume 7. Dordrecht: Redel.

Scribner, S. and Cole, M.
1981 *The Psychology of Literacy*. Cambridge, Mass.: Harvard University Press.

Sennett, R.
1977 *The Fall of Public Man*. New York: Knopf.

Serres, M.
1979 "The Algebra of Literature: the wolf's game." In J. V. Harari (ed.) *Textual Strategies*. Ithaca, N.Y: Cornell University Press.

1982 *The Parasite*. Baltimore: Johns Hopkins University Press.

Shapiro, M. J.
1981 *Language and Political Understanding : the politics of discursive practices*. New Haven: Yale University Press.

Sherwood, R.
1980 *The Psychodynamics of Race: vicious and benign spirals*. Brighton, Sussex: Harvester Press.

Shweder, R. A.
1980 "Rethinking Culture and Personality Theory Part III: from genesis and typology to hermeneutics and dynamics." *Ethos* 8: 60-94.

Shweder, R. A. and LeVine R. A. (eds.)
1984 *Culture Theory: essays on mind, self, and emotion.* New York: Cambridge Unversity Press.

Skinner, E. P.
1982 "The Dialectic Between Diasporas and Homelands." In J. E. Harris (ed.), *Global Dimensions of the African Diaspora.* Washington, D.C.: Howard University Press.

Snowden, F.
1983 *Before Color Prejudice: the ancient view of blacks.* Washington, D.C.: Howard University Press.

Snyder, M.
1981 "On the Self-Perpetuating Nature of Social Stereotypes. In D. L. Hamilton (ed.), *Cognitive Processes in Stereotyping and Intergroup Behavior.* Hillside, N.J.: Lawrence Erlbaum Associates.

Sowande, F.
1974 "The Quest of an African World View: the utilization of African discourse." In J. L. Daniel (ed.), *Black Comunication: dimensions of research and instruction.* Speech Comunication Association.

Sowell, T.
1981 *Ethnic America.* New York: Basic Books.

Soyinka, W.
1984 "The Fourth Dimension." *Semiotext(e)* 4, 3: 61–67.

References

Stack, C.
1974 *All Our Kin*. New York: Harper and Row.

Stack, J., Jr.
1981 *Ethnic Identities in a Transnational World*. Westport, Ct.: Greenwood Press.

Stember, C. H.
1976 *Sexual Racism*. New York: Elsevier.

Stourdze, Y.
1980 "The Status of the Human Operator in Comunication Systems." *International Journal of Social Science*, 32, 2: 53–67.

Sudarkasa, N.
1981 "Interpreting the African Heritage in Afro-American Family Organization." In H. P. McAdoo (ed.), *Black Families*. Beverley Hills: Sage Publications.

Swan, L. A.
1981 *Survival and Progress*. Westport, Ct.: Greenwood Press.

Taussig, M.
1984 "Culture of Terror—Space of Death: Roger Casement's Putumayo Report and the Explanation of Torture." *Comparative Studies in Society and History* 26, 3: 467-497.

Taylor, M.
1984 *Erring*. Chicago: University of Chicago Press.

Thomas, A. and Sillen, S.
1972 Racism and Psychiatry. New York: Brunner/Mazel.

Thompson, R. F.
1983 *Flash of the Spirit*. New York: Random House.

Todorov, T.
1984a *The Conquest of America: the question of the other*. New York: Harper and Row.

1984b *Mikhail Bakhtin: the dialogic principle*. Minneapolis: University of Minnesota Press.

Triandis, H.
1976 *Variations in Black and White: Conceptions of the Social Environment*. Urbana, Ill.: University of Illinois Press.

Turner, J. H. and Singleton, R. Jr.
1978 "A Theory of Ethnic Oppression: toward a reintegration of cultural and structural concepts in ethnic relations theory." *Social Issues* 56, 4: 10001-10019.

Tyler, S.
1984 "The Vision Quest in the West or What the Mind's Eye Sees." *Journal of Anthropological Research* 40, 1: 23-40.

Uya, O. E.
1982 "Conceptualizing Afro-American/African Realities." In J. E. Harris (ed.) *Global Dimensions of the African Diaspora*. Washington, D.C.: Howard University Press.

Vansine, J.
1982 "Mwasi's Trials." *Daedalus* 11, 2: 49–70.

Wagner, R.
1981 *The Invention of Culture*. Chicago: University of Chicago Press.

Walvin, J.
1976 *Black and White: The Negro in English Society 1555–1945*. London: Allen Lane.

Waugh, E.
1960 *Black Mischief*. Boston: Little, Brown, and Company.

245

References

Webber, T. L.
1978 *Deep Like the Rivers*. New York: Norton

Weitz, S.
1972 "Attitude, Voice, and Behavior: a repressed affect model of interracial interaction." *Journal of Experimental Social Psychology* 10: 109–120.

Wellman, D. T.
1977 *Portraits of White Racism*. New York: Cambridge University Press.

White, H.
1978 *Tropics of Discourse: essays in cultural criticism*. Baltimore: Johns Hopkns University Press.

White, J. L.; Parham, W. D.; and Parham, T. A.
1980 "Black Psychology: The Afro-American Tradition as a Unifying Force for Traditional Psychology." In R. Jones (ed.), *Black Psychology*. Second edition. New York: Harper and Row.

Whitten, N. E. and Szwed, J. (eds.)
1970 *Afro-American Anthropology*. New York: Free Press.

Williamson, J.
1984 *New People: miscegenation and mulattoes in the United States*. New York: New York University Press.

Wilson, W. J.
1978 *The Declining Significance of Race*. Chicago: University of Chicago Press.

Wirendu, K.
1976 "How Not to Compare African Thought with Western Thought." *Ch'indaba* 1, 2: 37-45.

Witkin, H. A.
   1978 *Cognitive Styles in Personal and Cultural Adaptation.* Worcester, Mass.: Clark University Press.

Witkin, H. A. and Berry, J. W.
   1975 "Psychological Differentiation in Cross-Cultural Perspective." *Journal of Cross-Cultural Psychology* 6: 4–87.

Wright, R. A., II.
   1979 "Investigating African Philosophy." In R. A. Wright II, (ed.), *African Philosophy.* Washington, DC: University Press of America.

Wyne, M. D.; White, K. P.; and Coop, R. H.
   1974 *The Black Self.* Englewood Cliffs, N.J.: Prentice-Hall.

Zahan, D.
   1979 *The Religion, Spirituality, and Thought of Traditional Africa.* Chicago: University of Chicago Press.

Additional AUTONOMEDIA Titles of Interest

MARX BEYOND MARX:
Lessons on the Gründrisse
Antonio Negri
A key figure in the Italian "Autonomia" Movement
reads Marx's *Grundrisse,* developing the critical and
controversial theoretical apparatus that informs the
"refusal of work" strategy and many other elements so
crucial to this "heretical" tendency in Marxist theory.

MODEL CHILDREN:
My Soviet Summers at Artek
Paul Thorez
The son of long-time French Communist Party leader
Maurice Thorez recounts his post-war childhood
experiences ar Artek, the prestigious Crimean summer
camp for children of the Soviet elite, where he saw aspects
of Russian political culture rarely revealed to the West.

RETHINKING MARXISM:
Struggles in Marxist Theory
Stephen Resnick & Richard Wolff, Editors
Contributions from 25 leading Marxist economists and
political scientists, including Bettelheim, Mandel, Amin,
Miliband, Wallerstein, O'Connor, Payer, Gunder Frank,
Bowles and Gintis, Genovese, dedicated to the work of
Paul Sweezy, Harry Magdoff and the *Monthly Review*.

Additional AUTONOMEDIA Titles of Interest

TROTSKYISM AND MAOISM:
Theory and Practice in France and the U.S.
A. Belden Fields

An important examination of the critical heritage of
Trotsky and Mao in two Western national contexts,
focusing on the multitudinous parties and sects and
their positions on national and international issues,
racism, sexism, gay rights, and students movements.

FILM AND POLITICS IN THE THIRD WORLD
John D. H. Downing, Editor

The only anthology of its kind in English, with critical
articles on leading figures and national cinemas, analyses
of important films, political/aesthetic manifestoes, and
interviews with directors from Africa, China, India,
Turkey, Iran, the Arab World, Latin America, and more.

THE ARCANE OF REPRODUCTION:
Housework, Prostitution, Labor & Capital
Leopoldina Fortunati

One of Italy's leading feminist writers critiques
the traditional received Marxist categories for
understanding the nature of capitalism and capitalist
production and their effects on the "reproductive"
role of women's labor and bodies.

Additional AUTONOMEDIA Titles of Interest

CLIPPED COINS, ABUSED WORDS, CIVIL GOVERNMENT
John Locke's Philosophy of Money
Constantine George Caffentzis
Starting from an actual fiscal crisis induced by the "clipping" of coins by money pirates in 17th-century England, Caffentzis opens out into an innovative and provocative critique of John Locke's philosophy of money, his theories of language, and his theories of history and the state.

SCANDAL:
Essays in Islamic Heresy
Peter Lamborn Wilson
A search for the "poetic facts" of heresy in Islamic history, ranging from "sacred pederasty" in Persian sufism and forbidden imagery in Islamic art to the inner teachings of the Assassins, heretical influences on "Shiite terrorism", and the mystical uses of wine, opium and hashish.

HORSEXE:
Essay on Transsexuality
Catherine Millot
A study of transsexual desire, with chapters on the female drive in psychosis, SheMales, the sex of the angels, the Skoptzy sect of Eastern European transsexual *castrati,* sex-change operations, and much more, by the Lacanian psychoanalyst and professor at the University of Paris.

Additional AUTONOMEDIA Titles of Interest

ON ANARCHY AND SCHIZOANALYSIS
Rolando Perez, Jr.

Using the "anti-oedipal" insights of Gilles Deleuze and Félix Guattari's *Capitalism and Schizophrenia,* Perez argues for "anti-fascist strategies in everyday life," and reads philosophy, literature, films and popular culture to critique deep political sympathies and antagonisms.

THE PROMISE OF SOLIDARITY
Inside the Polish Workers' Movement
Jean-Yves Potel

An account of the heady days of the Polish workers' movement, tracing the development of the *Solidarnosc* union struggle from its origins in the Lenin shipyards at Gdansk through the period of state repression and control, as seen by the Eastern European correspondent of *Rouge.*

INDIANS OF THE AMERICAS:
Human Rights and Self-Determination
Roxanne Dunbar Ortiz

An important assessment of the struggles of indigenous peoples of the Americas against coercion and co-optation by intervening states and political apparatuses, with lengthy examples ranging from the plains of North America to the Sandinista/Mosquito battles in present-day Nicaragua.

Additional AUTONOMEDIA Titles of Interest

FATAL STRATEGIES
Jean Baudrillard
A major work by the controversial author *of Simulations,
In the Shadow of the Silent Majorities, Forget Foucault,
The Ecstasy of Communication, Critique of the Political
Economy of the Sign, Mirror of Production* and *America,*
assessing the failure of radical responses to postmodernity.

GOD AND PLASTIC SURGERY:
Marx, Nietzsche, Freud and the Obvious
Jeremy Barris
An unusual and intensive examination of the work of
the intellectual progenitors of contemporary Western
thought, with a battery of insights into how to and how
not to think, act, feel, eat, dress, dance, or make love, in
ways to provoke, upset, and transfigure modern culture.

CASSETTE MYTHOS:
Making Music at the Margins
Robin James, Editor
Essays, reports and manifestoes from the *real* musical
underground, where the new medium of the tape cassette
has made it possible for individuals and groups to produce
and distribute their own music in their own style, free of the
censoring, perception-clogging nets of cash and commerce.

And from Semiotext(e) / Autonomedia

SEMIOTEXT(E)'S FIRST DIRTY DOZEN
Jim Fleming & Sylvère Lotringer, Editors
The mammoth anthology reprinting selections from all
of the earliest twelve numbers of the infamous journal,
including writing by more than fifty contributors to issues
like *Polysexuality, Anti-Oedipus, Ego Traps, Oasis, Schizo-
Culture, Nietzsche's Return, The German Issue,* more.

SEMIOTEXT(E) SF
Edited by Rudy Rucker,
Robert Anton Wilson & Peter Lamborn Wilson
Designed by Mike Saenz
Writing from the nether regions of the modern science/
speculative fiction universe, altered states served up on
post-political platters, cyberpunkish, cybergnostic, by turns
filthy, mean and angry, freakish and foul, sensuous and
sexy, vile, visionary, and altogether beyond compromise.

SOVIETEXT(E)
Nancy Condee and Vladimir Padunov, Editors
Contemporary Soviet writers and artists contribute to an
autonomous examination of their country's surprising
recent cultural and political transformations, presenting
material well beyond the sedate, customary, officially
approved networks of either Russian or Western observers.